Six Keys to Life Mastery

Unlocking Life Skills for Successful Living

Todd Alan Cudaback

Life Chronicles Publishing

Give your life a voice!

http://www.mylifechronicles.org

Life Chronicles Publishing
ISBN-978-0998911410
ISBN-10:0998911410

Cover Design:

Life Chronicles Publishing

Life Chronicles Publishing Copyright © 2017

In Memory of

Karen Joyce
"Rest in peace my friend, you are sorely missed.
Until we meet again, know that these keys are carried with me every
day."

CONTENTS

Introduction...page 1

Acknowledgments... page 3

****

My Story: Part I...page 5

6 Life Mastery Keys, An Overview................................ page 13

Key 1: Intention... page 17

Key 2: Manifesting.. page 27

Key 3: Abundance... page 39

****

My Story: Part II..page 59

Key 4: Health.. page 71

Key 5: Love.. page 83

Key 6: Transformation... page 105

Introduction

"There is only one success:
To be able to spend your life in your own way."

~ Christopher Morley

I used to ask questions that fell flat: Why am I so down on myself? How do I shut off these constant thoughts? Why is every day so robotic and dreary? It's hard for me to believe that those ideas kick-started my day, but it explains why my days were full of challenges.

I did not have a success mindset.
I did not know where to go for guidance.
I did not trust that anyone would understand my story.

After three visits to alcohol recovery, I started to wake up. It would have made such a difference if the seeds to success had been planted at a young age. I was in my 40's before any authority figure talked to me about co-creating my life with an infinite power greater than myself. It never dawned on me that I had gifts and that I was born to share them.

Today I can honestly say that I know who I am. I know my gifts, and I am grateful that every morning I wake again to a new day. I also know what I am not, and I don't waste time doing things I'm not called to do. My understanding that I must own my gifts and co-create my life with a higher power helped me take action. I now understand that success happens when I give my time strictly to my gifts.

1

I am not a writer. I'm a speaker.
I'm not a follower. I'm a leader.
I'm not an employee. I am an employer.

I know how to kick-start, inspire, and follow through with important plans. If there is something I can't do, I find people to help me get it done. Even with this book...I found professionals to help me through. I do this because I understand mastery principles.

I have been told everywhere I go, "You have a voice!" I use my voice to inspire and awaken people to ask big questions and take action! I believe I was called to do so. But there were years when I was unsure of my gifts, and I felt separated from myself. Those years were fraught with obsessive thinking that resulted in misguided beliefs and addiction. I didn't know how to choose, how to decide, or how to respond. I didn't have the first clue how someone gained success unless they were born into success.

I had to sober up in order to show up.

The truth is, no one is born into success. People make up their mind to be successful, but they must have principles in place to keep moving each and every day. That's the life mastery way of living. I invite you to try it out.

In this book, you will read my experiences – the before and after – as they relate to common pitfalls of leaving addiction behind. I suggest you do what I did; pay attention to the keys and try them every chance you get. Make a commitment to your success. You are old enough to understand none of us are born with success, yet some of us will consciously choose success. The keys are in this book.

Acknowledgements

I am amazed when I think about all the amazing people from my life that have brought me to the very place "I Am" today. Every door that I have walked through, all the stoplights that I have stopped at, every corner that I have turned, and every person that I have met. All of it has led me here, writing this acknowledgment.

This book documents a portion of small snippets of time during my life mastery journey. Two people come to mind who entered my life at the perfect time and help to guide me to an awakening and an understanding of my true self -- the person that I was always meant to be.

Mary Manin Morrissey is the person that came into this world with some talents and gifts that were meant to compliment the world around us. She showed up on the scene at a time of great desperation in my life. As well, her journey at that time was very challenging and filled her soul with great change. I can remember thinking that if she can weather this, there is no reason that I cannot overcome my challenges. She taught me the basics of metaphysics and introduced me to "New Thought" ideas that instantly helped me see the world from a different perspective. She introduced me to some of the teachings that have been around for a very long time, all of which helped me fit into and understand my world a little better.

The concept of a higher power and how I could trust that higher power to guide me in my daily affairs was a big deal for me. Alan Cohen was introduced to me by Mary. Alan taught me more concepts about my heart and how to connect to it. Through both teachers, I began to wake up to an awareness that was making a huge difference. Their leadership, wisdom, and teachings showed me a way of being, thinking, and showing up in the world that created a sense of real magic -- a magic that allowed me to create, BE and DO anything that I applied their teachings too.
A wizard was born! I see myself as a modern-day wizard versed in the art of dynamic alchemy, changing a dull dinging unguided life into a

3

bright shiny existence with a passion to light the way for others. This lead me to an understanding of my purpose as a servant leader.

Ten years ago, when I first wrote down my purpose, I did not understand it's meaning completely. I wrote: "My purpose is to help light the path that leads others to the fire that sparks a fire in their hearts." This purpose has guided me to some amazing discoveries about myself, and some gifts that I had no idea were inside of me. This book is about some of my discoveries and gifts, my trials and tribulations that lead me deeper along my path. Every decision that I have made has brought me to this place, and I have to tell you that because of it, I'm feeling 100 percent groovy. I say hello to the lamppost every day.

Please enjoy this book. Many people have helped me create it. It's me, it's from my heart, and it is my vision that you will use it to plant seeds in your being and reap huge benefits along your life mastery journey.

A BIG SHOUT OUT to Debby and Denise for helping me share this with you.

MY STORY

PART 1

Even the Boy Scouts have figured it out: Be prepared.

--United States Marines Corps

I was raised to be a man's man, a strong farm hand, and basically an ordinary tough guy. My Dad influenced me powerfully. He grew up in a masculine world in middle America where he was a big football fan and raised to be a corn farmer. He coached me in football, baseball, basketball, and soccer when I was a just a kid. If I got hurt while playing, I was told, "Shake it off!" And, "Big boys don't cry!" Every injury was met with another chance to be tough as nails. These messages were hammered into my brain and my body. Consequently, I became completely closed off from my feelings.

This was one of my first agreements in life: Real men don't feel. I didn't like it, but it was a concept straight from my dad, and it was all he knew. The boy scouts enforced it even more, and later came the game of hunting wild animals — something I was not keen on — but these messages came from men I looked up to. They were teaching me how to be a man's man, as this was all they knew.

I was only 11 when my uncle introduced me to booze, and I liked it! I liked the way it made me feel. I drank so much I got super intoxicated. As the days pressed on, I could count on my uncle feeding this magic stuff to me, and every time, I had the same reaction; I felt great! Alcohol gave me the permission to feel superhuman! This was the stuff, man!

Up until now, the only feelings I ever saw a man express was anger. I noticed that when men got angry, they got their way. It worked for me, too. I could throw a tantrum and get what I wanted. At age 12, my folks divorced and I spent a lot of time feeling upset. The only other option I knew was too numb out and try to feel nothing at all. So now I had a new agreement: I could feel angry, or I could add a little alcohol and feel good. Every chance I got, I chose the latter.

My parent's divorce was a battle, and my dad remained emotionally detached. Even though I hung out with him and went to his house on weekends, I withdrew, too. We would build things together, but we rarely talked about anything. I had no one to relate to. At my mom's house, I had a new step-dad who was a Marine, a woodsman, and a hunter, and he held the same tough standards I had been raised to understand. I became an angry, enraged, and misdirected youth.

Sensing my detachment from people and everything else, my mom took me to see a psychologist. I remember sitting sullen and quiet, like a bump on a log throughout the entire session. The therapist was trying to get me to open up. However, I was tough and seething with rage at the fact I had been brought to him for some kind of rehab.

He looked at me at one point and said, "Your mom tells me you have a great, big backyard. Have you ever considered doing something like growing flowers?" The therapist's words hit me like a Mack truck. I thought to myself that he couldn't be serious. *Grow flowers?* That was the stupidest idea I'd ever heard. I got in my mom's car afterward and said,

"That's it! I'm never going back to this dude. He wants me to 'freakin' grow flowers!!" She never took me back.

Now I had a new agreement: *You don't have to listen to anybody.* But this was one of the first agreements that sprung from personal inertia. The previous agreements were influenced heavily by an unfair world and withdrawn father-figures. Walking out of that office, I felt a strong sense of my own will and my power.

I was much too young to understand that I was only 16 and not yet a man. I was rebellious as heck. The problem was that being drunk was mighty debilitating. And this is when I was introduced to marijuana. Smoking weed let me function and allowed me to feel good! Problem solved! By now, I had a few buddies who also liked getting high, so we smoked in between class breaks at the high school. It felt good, but the affects wore off too quickly so we'd have to smoke more. And more!

Next thing you know, we were old enough to drive! I did not play by the rules, and pretty soon, the Everett police knew me on a first-name basis. My life seemed pointed in the wrong direction with no goals, hopes or aspirations. My best friend, Don, made a big life decision that seemed wise to me, so I followed his lead.

At 17, I left home to join the Marines and see the world. At this time, I had no money, no sobriety, and no boundaries. I wasn't unlike my uncles or cousins who went before me – drinking too much and thinking I could get away with anything. Joining the Marines was a second chance to wise up. Not knowing what I was in for, and after my first week, I learned that no one gets to walk out or say, "I've had enough." Nothing was on my terms, and this sent me to my cot more than once in a pool of tears.

Boot camp was hard, demeaning, degrading, full of discipline, and full of structure. The Marines were teaching me that I could do so much more than I thought I could. In fact, this lesson was pounded into every part of my being. One day in the hottest weather and fully uniformed, we were instructed to run this long obstacle course. Oh man!! I felt every bit of the challenge in my lungs, my feet, my back – but I also knew there was a finish line. I had to make it to the finish line! I kept this playing over and over in my mind – just get to the end. Those last few steps were such a relief. And then I heard the dreaded words from the commanding officer, "Ok, let's see you do it again." I was shocked! He couldn't really mean it, could he? But my short experience with the Marines told me that he meant it and that there'd be no stalling to think about it. "Go! Now!"

That was boot camp. If we weren't running our legs off, we might be back in the barracks learning a whole new definition of "clean." I had never starched a shirt. I hardly ever made my bed, ever, before the Marines. Now I had to dust and spic-n-span my bathroom. I didn't value these things, but I came to understand that the Marines valued structure just as much as they valued applying force to get the job done. "Take that hill!" This was the brute force of the Marines. Once I got over the fact that I could not go home and quit, I slowly started to see a positive side to all the hard work.

The Marines were teaching me a vocation, too. And a philosophy. We worked during the day – gave it everything we had -- and then we'd go out and get drunk. Night after night, we'd drink up the place, and if our shirts were pressed and shoes were shined by morning, all was well.

Surprisingly, I managed to get married while in the Marines. The primary reason for getting married was so I could live "off base." My wife and I were practically strangers and the relationship was fraught with challenges. I didn't know how to love and care for myself, and I certainly didn't know how to think about another person.

And then one day, my arrogance caught up with me. For drinking and driving recklessly, I was ordered by the Marine Corps to undergo an intensive four-week alcohol treatment program. I was just 22, and I didn't go willingly. I had hit a squad car which resulted in an injury to a police officer. The treatment plan helped me get off alcohol and marijuana temporarily. Even though I wasn't drinking or using drugs for several months, I still had lots of bottled up anger inside and I certainly wasn't in touch with my emotions. In fact, I rarely thought about the damage I had caused to the officer, or anyone.

Instead of learning to be accountable, I made a new agreement: Life is more fun when you are not getting caught. I ran with this idea for a while. But Alcoholics Anonymous (AA) was putting a real cramp in my style. I was under the misguided thought that I could do whatever I wanted and on my own. Though I stayed away from alcohol, I was back to smoking pot, and eventually reached a point where I couldn't smoke enough to feel high.

It became clear that I had to bring alcohol into the picture to ensure a solid block from feeling anxious. I spent more time out with my buddies drinking than at home and my wife finally left me. Had I been in touch with my feelings, I might have experienced the impact of her being gone, but I was right back in the tavern without missing a beat.

After a long lapse away from Alcoholics Anonymous, I could barely remember the wisdom they had bestowed. It was almost as if it had never happened. The treatment didn't stick because I didn't want it bad enough. I was brewing up a future completely fraught with crisis and mind-screwing games. I had no insight that I needed to get out of my own way.

I knew how to work hard – that was drilled into my being – so I went to Alaska and signed my summer away in exchange for a fat paycheck and more manly-man job experience. Maybe I was searching for answers because one came wrapped as a book the day I left home for Alaska. I was in the airport bookstore and on a total whim, I stopped and focused on the picture of a featured book. It was Mary Manin Morrissey, a speaker for the Unity Church. I knew nothing more than what I saw -- a sensational smile. Her book was titled, *Building Your Fields of Dreams*. I had several hours of nothing to do but stare out the window at 30,000 feet. So, I bought the book and devoured it on that flight. I had no idea at the time that her book was planting the seeds for my transformation, one that I would postpone until age 42.

I had a lot more drinking and gambling with fate to get out of my system. In my late twenties, I married a second time to the daughter of my favorite tavern owner. In this marriage, I fathered three daughters. After a decade, I was divorced again because my world had become an endless series of days; I'd wake up hung over, work my tail off, get drunk, and pass out till the next morning.

This was what I knew. Alcoholism was running my life story.

6 Life Mastery Keys:
An Overview

You don't know *how* you don't want to be until you get there.

I wish someone had said this to me when I was coming of age. There was no handbook on how to be, and no one talked about living your life on purpose. The truth was that it was so easy to get side tracked and so hard to get back on course. For me, it took three rounds of treatment before I created this mantra to remind myself that the old ways will never work. Drinking doesn't work. Lying doesn't work. Being the center of attention doesn't work. All that behavior paved one dead end after another.

As a kid, it made no sense to me that the US was drilling for oil where hell was and shooting rockets high in the sky, putting men into space out where heaven existed. Raised Presbyterian, it seemed completely nonsensical. No one explained why God wanted this. I had an understanding there was something more – a Source I would get to know better over time – but as a kid, there was a lot of mystery around the topic of God. I was very curious to know how everything in the universe fit together.

Like so many kids, I came into this world with wonder and thirst, and over those first 20 years, a lot of that energy got driven out. The primary words that really stuck were, "You can't do that," and "You're not good enough for that." Robert Holden and Louise Hay discovered in their research for the book, *Life Loves You*, "Children hear the word 'no' up to 400 times a day, and that some children learn this word before saying 'mommy' or 'daddy.'" How does that get a child ready for life if the number one word is, no?

I had questions about the world and no sense of where to look for direction. Who can I trust? How do I deal with my non-stop mind chattering? What if I start a cool plan and then end up failing?

The mind is so powerful. I have let my mind take me down some pretty rebellious roads. I had an understanding that my mind is a fertile ground for ideas, but it was not until I read Mary Manin Morrissey's book, *Building Your Field of Dreams*, that seeds for spiritually growth were finally planted. It was the first and only book about spirituality that I ever cared to write my name in. In the book, I read about the Law of Attraction, Intuition, Abundance – all concepts that metaphysicians had practiced for centuries. My mind hummed with these ideas for nearly a decade before I got serious and put them into practice.

I can clearly remember the moment my relationship with my mind changed. I was in my 40's walking across a regular street on a regular day, and I realized: I can choose my thoughts. Every single moment, I am given another opportunity to choose how I think about things and what I will do right now. I don't get everything right all the

14

time, and I constantly remind myself to be alert. After all, you don't know how you don't want to be until you get there.

AN OVERVIEW OF THE SIX KEYS

Intention - to focus on a vision that will lead toward your dream.

Manifesting - to passionately take action toward your dream and hold the vision.

Abundance - to believe you deserve your dream by being receptive and aligned.

Health - to live a clean, uncluttered life.

Love - to master acceptance and harmony.

Transformation - to be one with the changes and calling meant for you.

The GRAND key of all - the practice of gratitude.

Before you go any further, make a commitment right now to your dream. See it as a vision with your mind's eye and hold it, focus on it, and dedicate yourself to seeing it into fruition. You can have your dream. Just like my sponsor once said to me, *I will believe in you until you can believe in yourself.*

Life Mastery Key

#1

Intention

"What you get by achieving your goals is not as important as what you

become by achieving your goals."

--Zig Ziglar

Life mastery keys are from the spiritual laws of the universe that support you on the path to your dream. Based on my story, you know you don't have to be born into wealth and or have a perfect record to manifest your dreams. You have to wake up, clean up, and show up. I came to understand this truth in my middle age, and I want to share what I know so that you can get going without brutal and painful lessons. I sincerely believe you do not have to hit bottom in order to wake up to a magical life.

As you set intentions and truly believe in them, you will achieve your dreams or you will achieve something even better. Your intention has to be believable. Without the belief, you're working with fantasy.

Masterful and alternative medicine advocate, Deepak Chopra, understands and articulates intention as follows:

Intention is the starting point of every dream. It is the creative power that fulfills all your needs, whether for money, relationship, spiritual awakening or love.

Intentional mastery can be summed up as a marriage of joining your dream with your focused vision. The two come together and make something beautiful and perfect for you. Your intention is deeply connected to a purpose you will live out because you were called to do so.

STARTING EVERETT HYDRAULICS

When you are intentional, you are moving energy. The laws of the universe *follow* your mind's capacity. The action follows the thoughts, bringing a myriad of opportunities, ideas, people or facts into your awareness. Have you ever been told to be careful what you are thinking about? This is why! Thoughts have power because thoughts lead us toward action.

Mary's book helped plant important seeds about my future, namely that I wanted to have my own hydraulic shop. I was working at another shop for an owner who seemed burned out and I felt it was time to venture on, but I didn't know how. On a lunch break, I read an article in an industrial publication about a place called Baltimore Hydraulics. In the article, the writer described everything I thought I'd like my "new" shop to offer down to a tee. I cut the article out, blew it up, and affixed it to my wall. I looked at the article every day. Within a few weeks, and much to my surprise, things began to change. First, the owner I worked for sold the shop. I didn't want to start up with a new boss, so I left too, but I got plenty of calls to do side jobs. It was clear that the customers liked my work, so I got the idea to sit down and write out the details of a new shop much like the one I from the article. I didn't really know the depth of my dream until the details made contact with paper and I saw my design unfolding.

I found a location and many of the customers from the old shop followed, as did some of the essential workers. I didn't know how much energy and belief to invest in my intention, but I followed practical advice as well as the principles I had read in *Building Your Field of Dreams*. There were leaps of faith, and there were hard, practical decisions to make.

Most business plan models are a lot of blue sky thinking along with your best hunch. *Can you guess where you'll be three years from now? Five years from now?* I projected sales numbers for the next five years and the bank helped out with a start-up loan. My little hydraulic shop began growing up around me. I started incorporating those ideas from the article and my written design.

Five or six years later I looked around and realized what I created was a version of Baltimore Hydraulics. I pulled out the business plan and realized for the first three years, I had hit my forecasted numbers almost exactly. Honestly, it was practically to the number. Intentional mastery was doing its work because I had not looked at the numbers for several years. I had a plan in a desk drawer and an article on the wall. No coaches or silver spoons to carry me through. When I fished the plan that was in the drawer and looked, the numbers were so close to my wild guesses that I got goose bumps! I had to show up and do the work, but it wasn't a struggle. I had a plan that aligned with my values and skills. Everything fell into place in its own time.

START EACH DAY INTENTIONALLY

Intentional mastery is a skill that keeps you awake and on-purpose each day of your life. It starts the moment you open your eyes in the morning and greet your day. Think about it: do you have particular patterns for starting your day? I begin every day early and ready to go! I don't linger in bed wishing the day will disappear. I get up with the intention to have a great day. I was taught a very simple mantra that keeps me on track: "Pay attention to what you're paying attention to." It's easy. I ask myself: Are the things I'm thinking about enlivening my day or getting in my way? Anything we do or think about can get in the way if we give it all our attention. Just grasping that idea allowed me to stop spinning negative thoughts about the past or fretting anxious thoughts regarding the future. Without these knee-jerk reactions to thoughts, you, too, can focus on what's happening in the present moment.

When you send a message of what you intend to be, do, or have, you're communicating powerfully with your greatest source of energy. You're aligning with your core values and purpose. And that high-quality alignment moves an idea forward. One the one hand, it's a powerful concept, and yet it's also really simple. But if there is no one there to teach you, how will you know about these spiritual laws? The real cool part is that these laws are at work all the time. As I became willing to take decisive action in my life and not numb out with alcohol, the law of Intentional mastery began to unfold.

When you are in touch with your values and not overcomplicating things, that which you intend has space to grow. But let me remind you: It is *not* the people sleeping in or wishing for a lucky break who live intentionally. Setting an intention means stating what you want. Anything you focus on and believe in has no choice but to come into being. It may not manifest in the exact form that you conjured in your mind. But then again, if you are really clear, it likely will!

Mary's book outlined how important it is to be very focused, uncluttered, and in a state where you truly believe you deserve your intention. Don't worry about what others profess you should or should not have; what do you intend to have? Get into the details. For me, it was a business. Others might desire a family in the next three years, but be clear so that you manifest a family of babies and not a family of puppies or giraffes. I started out with a big pad of unlined paper and wrote out what I saw in my mind – in both pictures and words – and I didn't leave anything out.

THE BLOCKS TO A DREAM

Your past, as well as your parent's history, can influence your thinking without your awareness. This was often the case for me. A sure and fast way to break free of old patterns is to speak your new idea – say it out loud. Mary suggested that each phrase of doubt be re-framed by beginning with, "Up until now…." It's not hard to do. Think of something you have beaten yourself up about or that you have heard your folks shame themselves over. Have the courage to re-write it:

- Up until now, I have struggled to manage my bills, but I am determined to record my spending and use a realistic budget.

- Up until now, I have quit jobs that caused me any anxiety, but now I am ready to go to school and re-tool my skill set.

- Up until now, I have procrastinated about getting into shape, but that doesn't mean I can't start swim lessons today.

Maybe you're a member of an organization where you could ask for help. Do you have social networking connections to whom you could reach out? The possibilities are limitless. Since people love helping others, providing help makes them feel useful and appreciated. When you ask for help, the world almost magically opens to your intention. You will find that setting your intention will teach you to practice being honest and notice who is honest with you.

Meditate on these ideas:

- You must feel 100 percent safe knowing this person will support you and has your best interests at heart. If you have trust issues with the person, that will create a block and get in the way.

- Albert Einstein said, "every thought and every idea has been thought before." You usually don't tap into something totally new. It's just new to you. Even with new technology it's building on what's come before. Trust that you are being inspired to express the idea in your own way.

- Everything that ever was and ever will be is right here, right now. So why not ask for help? It's already out there -- you just need to pull it to you.

- Ask for support from people who either have more skill than you or who want to handle what you don't want to do. I hire people who are good at tasks I don't want to fuss over. That saves energy so I can be available to things that are a good match to my skills and desires.

DESIGN YOUR INTENTION ACCELERATOR

It's especially important to stay focused on your dreams because persuasive people will want you to buy into *their* intentions. This will set you out of your high vibration and off course. You may notice successful people advancing with their idea, leading you to fall into a spell of false beliefs, such as, "They must have a better plan!" When you ask them questions, you might decide their values around happiness are not necessarily aligned with your idea of happiness. Once you determine your intention, allow all the other eye-catching thoughts to remain in your periphery.

I did that recently with a good friend I hadn't seen in a while, who wanted me to get involved with a network marketing company for a line of water filtration machines that cost $4,000 each. People are crawling over themselves to get these machines. I said, "You're a great salesman and it may be a wonderful product, but I'm not passionate about it. I'm not passionate about being in a multilevel marketing company either. I wish you the best of luck."

24

I have learned that it is best when choosing not to accept a request, communicate by validating the person, understanding they have a desired intention, and gently decline. I never aim to discredit them because they're pursuing something that fulfills their ideals. If they continue to try to sell me something, I let them know it's not my game and thanks anyway.

If you really can't decide whether to follow a friend's intention, go back to the details of your dreams. You wrote them down for this very reason -- they provide a crystal-clear picture of your focused plan. You see, these intentions are setting you up to manifest an abundant life. You want to bring into existence the life you were intended to lead, not the life someone else has dreamt up with their dose of passion and their core values. That's why this first key is so critical – the law of attraction brings things into being whether it is your first choice or your friend's first choice. Focus on your own to achieve greater happiness.

Life Mastery Key

#2

Manifesting

We cannot solve our problems with the same thinking we used when we created them.

-- Albert Einstein

I suggest if you do not currently own a book by the great Dr. Wayne Dyer that you pick one up. He wrote, *The Power of Intention*, a great place to start. Here's his take on manifesting:

It is the art of getting what you want…If you want to manifest your dreams, you must become a master at monitoring the thoughts and feelings you are aligning with. Your thoughts and feelings become your reality, so become adept at observing the thoughts and feelings you are creating for yourself.

Expanding on your very own and intentional vision requires a form of prayer that in no way needs to be religious. The Laws of Attraction and Abundance take over when we align to a vibration that is already at work. Consider that this sort of prayer is a way of taping into your wisdom and also releases control at the same time. Just as a mother puts her faith in her child's ability to place one foot after another and masterfully learn to walk, we must be willing to take steps, too. In this process of your prayer, get quiet, close your eyes, and be receptive to hearing answers. Your goal is to focus on your intention and ask:

- "What is it that I'm to know?"
- If you get answers but still need clarity ask yourself, "Is this it? Or not it?"
- Then simply ask, "Is there more for me to know?

As you listen, you are connecting with not only your intention, but also your purpose. No one comes into the world without some important purpose to fulfill for either their family, their community or

28

the world. We are all meant to contribute by using our skills. Whenever you are setting an intention, it is best to have your purpose guiding you.

THE ANCIENT SYSTEM OF MANIFESTING

Manifesting has been taught for thousands of years. It's certainly not a new idea. Yet you might be wondering why you were not taught meditation and how to manifest your dreams in your high school curriculum? I believe it's because hundreds of years ago organized religion played an important role, taking away anything that empowered people to think independently and run their own lives. Religious leaders needed a way to control the masses. Consider the witch hunts that took place over two hundred years ago. People with natural intuitive abilities were hunted down, imprisoned, or killed by church leaders. Also, kings and rulers played a part in keeping people from believing in their ability to manifest.

You may have heard, "You'll get your reward in heaven." The flip side of that statement was implied with, "if you don't do it our way, you'll go to hell." The Kings in ancient Europe said this to keep the majority of the population working and slaving away to pay taxes to the King. They instilled fear and people lived their entire lives and died with the idea they would receive no reward now, but they'll get it after death in heaven.

Now we know better. We have a myriad of choices and the ability to empower ourselves and live a life of meaning, purpose, joy, and abundance. Knowing you have choices means you have the power to create the life you want through the Life Mastery Key of manifesting. The power of your thoughts can create Heaven or Hell right here on earth. Consider:

- Choosing Hell means you choose an experience that includes disappointment, blame, anger, resentment, and other negative emotional states when things happen in your life. It also means choosing a low energetic vibrational state.

- Choosing Heaven means you choose an experience that includes joy, openness, curiosity, laughter, wisdom, and other positive emotional states and a high energetic vibrational state. It means looking for the gift or lesson in every experience.

The more you work with these abilities given to you by your Source, the more you'll have the power to manifest what you want to create -- a life of purpose and prosperity. Letting go of what doesn't work, including the tendency to try to control everything, you allow the space for more good to come into your experience.

GIVE IT ALL THE ENERGY IT TAKES

Be committed to watching and shifting your negative thoughts to positive ones. If you want to experience a remarkable life, you can't allow negativity to take over your thoughts. Expand all the energy you need to become aware, present, focused, and upbeat as much as possible.

When you set your intention, and you are truly clear, hold that picture in your mind and allow space for the dream to grow. It's not necessary to focus on the how, the why, or start asking, "What do I do next?" Just by creating your vision, you are making space for a dream to take shape. You want to put your faith in your ability to follow that path and avoid destructive thinking, such as:

- Why isn't it happening yet?
- Did I do something wrong?
- Should I start over?
- Is it too complicated?
- Don't I deserve to have this dream?

When you ask questions like these, you send out a low vibration, or a low energy which will keep you in a state of longing. Instead, build your intention, infuse it with positive high-vibration! Remember to revisit the vision. I have found this to be a great way to anchor a positive mindset. Say affirmations, such as, "I know it's coming soon." Don't ponder on why it hasn't manifested and think, "It's not happening fast enough." Here's the key: it will manifest what you intended. Or, it will manifest something better.

There are 24 hours in each a day and only eight of those hours are for sleeping. So, if you work for eight hours, you have another six to eight hours daily to focus on an activity that gives you sustenance. You have a wide swath of time to explore ways not to be a couch potato. You might want to investigate a business idea, a hobby you love or an adventure of some type like hiking the Oregon Trail or learning to paint.

I suggest splitting your life into chunks. You may use that six to eight hours you're not sleeping or working to pursue education or something which provides growth intellectually, emotionally or spiritually. Every morning when I get up I read something uplifting. It gives me essential brain food I can chew on all day. Some days I'll choose to read an inspirational book. Or, I visualize what I want to create for the day in the morning. That's another way of expending a little more energy dedicating yourself to your personal growth and getting in a groove that provides food for learning. It gives your mind inspiring ideas to mull over rather than pondering every decision to death. I can go through my entire day without remembering what I read in the morning, but my subconscious mind is cogitating on a thought or concept.

When your subconscious works on an idea, it might seem like it goes dormant for a while. Then you find yourself implementing it and asking to yourself, "Where did that come from?" It seems like it came from out of the blue. You never know where that "blue place" is, but that's how new thoughts spring forth. You planted the seed and it burst into bloom at the moment you needed it.

DON'T WASTE TIME ON THOUGHTLESS IDEAS

So much time is wasted on thoughts like, "I wonder what would happen if that dog bit that guy." Our minds can be entertained all day with misdirected thoughts, hypothetical notions and useless worry. Fully 99 percent of our problems are created in our mind and they're not even real. You can't even put them in a paper bag and throw them away.

When the coffeemaker won't turn on or your shoelace breaks, those are problems you can deal with in any given moment. However, a great deal of time and energy is wasted on thoughtless thoughts about what someone else might think. To live an amazing life, our minds can't be bogged down with thoughtless thoughts. So, make a commitment to pay attention to when they spring up in your mind. When you do you'll change the quality of your thinking, especially if you were thinking and musing negatively before. Gossip, worry, and fear are more examples of thoughtless thoughts millions of people obsess about endlessly.

This is your time! Your life is ticking away every second. Make a commitment to live on purpose and not give your day away to thoughtless ideas.

MODERN DAY MANIFESTING

When I end each episode of my radio show, I always offer my listeners the same farewell: *Make it a great day! It's all about choice.* I say this every single time because I believe it! The power of manifesting is about getting your mindset in tune so that you are clear and focused. At this point, you are set up to make awesome decisions and manifest your dreams.

As you discovered in my story of abusing alcohol and marijuana, I used to have a very different mindset. I did what I wanted when I wanted. You might think manifesting is like that – just launching yourself forward any 'ol way you feel like it. The truth is that manifesting is a training of the mind.

You are basically clearing the space for the mystery to unfold. I was hungry to "start manifesting" a great business after I finished rehab. I wanted to crack the code and I tried hard, twisting my mind in knots for the next and best idea. Everything I was told and everything I read seemed to say, "Things will appear in your life magically." So, I tried to push it and force the issue, and when it didn't work, I wondered, "What's the deal here?"

The more I lunged toward success, the less I saw results. I'd study, stay up late, draw up more plans, but it seemed like I was spinning. Remember, I was raised a worker, believing in sheer force and brute horsepower. That was how I was trained to get things done. Eventually I realized I needed to chill out and let go of the workhorse mindset.

The biggest key to shifting your mindset to a healthy, manifesting generator is to commit to your inner work. We all have an "inside job" to attend to if we expect to get out of auto-pilot. Ask yourself where you are holding on to old resentment, anger, blame, and other negative thoughts. Wayne Dyer often used to ask his audiences, "Who is taking up free rent in your mind?" When you've stripped away all this nonsense, you have a clean breeding ground for pure happiness.

Daily, you must commit to staying focused on your dreams because that's what going to make you happy. Everyone has the ability to create intentions, desires, and dreams of what they want. It is tempting to forget that we are all set up to live a magical life from the inside out. But it is a practice. In order to manifest a dream, you cannot let passing thoughts take over, "Well, I don't have it yet, and I've been working hard." Negative emotions wipe out everything.

Pam Grout, the author of *E-Squared* says, "If we simply devote our minds to feeling rich, to being grateful for all the already-apparent riches in our lives—say, our families and our wonderful friends—being broke would disappear. We only experience it because we devote our thoughts to it. That's how powerful our minds are." I am a follower of Pam Grout's work because I believe in the energy and mindset she lives by and writes about in her books. She is the real deal.

What sort of devotion do you have in place? How does your day begin? I developed a relationship with my higher power and that is the fierce Source I allow to guide my every thought. In the old days, my AA sponsor called me out and said, "You don't truly want {INSERT YOUR DREAM} because you don't believe it." He was right. I had to develop a daily practice with myself consciously release my emotional blocks. I watched him believe in me until I could believe in myself. Over time, I noticed a switch; I was manifesting new experiences because I now believed in the possibility and took the action, without the crazy brute force, and things came to fruition.

Manifesting your dream is not the same energy you would use for tasks such as chopping wood, building an engine or sewing a dress. It's about aligning *your thinking* in the right way, with rigor and focus. I manifest new opportunities on a regular basis. I'll imagine a new truck, walk down the street, and there is a "For Sale" sign on the same model

I just imagined. Because I now believe in the possibilities, my desires almost effortlessly appear.

In 2006 a documentary movie called "The Secret" was seen by millions. Some loved and embraced it. Skeptics thought it was ridiculous. I believe "The Secret" forgot a critical step which led many to believe manifesting doesn't work. An essential step is that you must take action. Taking action gets you in the flow. You create the visions, dreams, and feelings as if it's already happening. I can't just think up a truck I want to buy and expect it to turn up in my driveway. Nothing happens if I don't act. Again, I like to come back to the AA principle that everything happens "one day at a time." You never want to force your life to go faster or get so angry that your dreams are not yet here, but you also have to be willing to stay focused on appropriate actions each day.

The ideas in *The Secret* certainly were not made up of phony-baloney. The problem was that my friends who followed the ideas literally did nothing to turn their dream into reality. Action must be taken. Having an intentional mindset is the very beginning of the journey, but it does not end there. You can't take a break before you even get going.

As I mentioned earlier, I started my machine shop in 1999 at a time when I had a lot to learn about manifesting a dream. My spiritual teacher, Mary Manin Morrissey wrote in her book, Building Your Field of Dreams:

The dream that you envision for your life is a gift. You cannot experience that gift unless you receive it. No matter how wondrous the bequest, to the person with hands clenched, the gifts remain unopened, unappreciated.

I believe it is through the power of manifesting that I have made it beyond some rocky economic times when other businesses like mine had to close their doors. I have always been able to make payroll and pay the bills. I have always had a positive cash flow. I have always been able to get the parts and equipment I want and need. I have had moments when things dipped, and I have used those moments to take further action and check in with my mind. Am I staying the course or have I slipped into "stinkin' thinkin"? Whenever I clean up my thoughts, no more than 48 hours pass before new customers have come through the door. I truly believe they show up because I visualize them coming in. I trust my higher power will give me strength because the shop is set up; we are here, ready and able! It's the best marketing strategy ever.

I often say that manifesting is actually a co-creation with Source. But first thing's first – do not neglect the healing work that allows you to tune in with a higher vibration. Then, notice how it's almost as if circumstances start lining up to give you what you want. Welcome joy and gratitude! How could you possibly be unhappy with those thoughts and ideas?

Consider that your highest Source wants you to succeed. Practice these five steps:

- Turn the transmitter on, get into a high-vibration state. That's the key to switch on the microphone so you're heard and acknowledged by Spirit. That means be and feel happy, grateful and harbor no residual negativity.

- Create your desire in detail. Set the intention that your desire is for good and it's in alignment with what you truly want.

- Take on the same feelings of gratitude and excitement as if you already had it in your life. Resonate with it and keep your positive feeling state going.

- Consciously and willing release any attachment to the outcome. Go on about your business still feeling that same sense of high vibration and gratitude. Remind yourself: "My Source is in change!"

- Finally, take action and do something which will allow you to *remain in the flow* of opportunity so it can come into your reality.

Life Mastery Key

#3

Abundance

*"True abundance is not based on your net worth,
it's based on your self-worth"*

~ Gabrielle Bernstien

When I was in early recovery, there were all kinds of terms and concepts new to me. One was this idea of abundance. Was it about wealth? Was it about designer clothes and fancy cars? I'd try to wrap my head around it, but I just wasn't getting it. My background had shown me that some people were born with it and others were not. Abundance was in the gray zone in between the black and white ideas – very foreign territory for me.

Marianne Williamson, spiritual author of *A Return to Love* says this about abundance, "The key to abundance is meeting limited circumstances with unlimited thoughts." I needed to see this law in action. Ironically, one day I was taking the elevator in my apartment building and noticed a smattering of used items. There were salt and pepper shakers and a couple of picture frames hanging out in the elevator, completely unattended and unclaimed. Later that day, they were gone. The next day, a pair of gloves and a scarf. Later that day, gone. Small items continued to appear and disappear. And then finally, the doors opened, and I caught her. A nice woman was setting up new items so I asked what she was up to. She was very timid at first, be she revealed that this is a practice of hers – a practice of abundance. I listened to her story and learned that as she cleared away nice and useful things from her life, she made physical and mental space for what she really wanted. She knew she deserved more and that her desires would manifest if she made an offering of the things that had served her. All of a sudden, I got it! And not in the exactly same way but with a similar frame of mind, I copied her.

First, I thought about things I was thankful to have owned or used, especially things I had taken good care of, and I thought of how they might be useful for others. First, I eliminated things I did not need any longer, and later I developed an appreciation that some things would be better appreciated in someone else's care. I remember when a friend of mine parted with her dog, a very protective Pitt-mix whom she loved deeply when she found out she was expecting a baby. She knew the dog needed devotion and she could not be nearly as available, nor did she want to risk that there were not enough hours in the day to give to a young dog and her new baby.

The law of abundance is about being in alignment energetically, and you simply can't if you have too much stuff and not enough time. Nothing new that you truly desire will find its way to you under these conditions. Today, I understand that clutter can be physical or emotion, spiritual or environmental. Clutter can also live in the mind. It clogs up the space I want to use for something more meaningful or more powerful, like a business, a relationship, or a new, and exciting hobby. Taking a little time and energy to attend to clutter sets the energy of abundance in motion. If you don't know where to start, it might be due to how little attention you are giving to your purpose and intentional mastery. You need to work with that very first key to literally make space for your abundant life.

A GOOD ATTITUDE IS BETTER THAN GREAT POSSESSIONS

Have you ever set aside a day to sort through your stuff? Easily, you may have had items on hand for years that no longer serve your higher values in any way. I understand that parting with some things can be tough. To be abundant, you must make space for the new creation. You are birthing a dream. It may take a few rounds of clearing things and waiting for the miracle to happen before your mind catches up.

It is essential that you create the mindset of abundance and also reframe the thoughts that sabotage you and result in lack. Devote time to developing new thoughts and new beliefs. Your openness will leave no room for thoughts of lack. That's when you'll notice a shift and flow. It's not about how much you can get. Instead, it's a matter of how much good can you handle. Be grateful for everything you have and everything coming your way and watch your life change!

PAUSE TO TAKE STOCK

How do you make the switch from being a person who speaks with judgments and sarcasm to becoming a person full of gratitude? It can feel silly at first because the current culture keeps us disconnected and out of tune. It seems cool to be unhappy, constantly feeling as though you don't have enough. Have you ever seen a picture of a hip-hop star posing with a bright smile? Of course not. It's not cool. Even with gold chains, diamond grills, and mansions, many people among the wealthy acquire grand objects and still look dissatisfied. Some of them are far from having an abundant mindset because they just don't know it's not about stuff.

You may have grown up believing that if you receive kindness, you're not independent. Perhaps being offered a gift quickly leaves you feeling uncomfortable, so you decline because self-pride takes over. You might say, "That's okay, I don't need it," but the gift-giver knew you do need it and wanted you to have it. Remember, you can't be shut down and open at the same time. In other words, declining an honest gift will not lead to abundance. Receive every gift big or small given with a kind heart because it makes: 1) the giver feels good, 2) you feel good and 3) the energy builds. All three pieces are important in any equation of abundance.

Take notice of the people who have moved up so fast. You know what they say: Easy come, easy go! I'm thinking about the fame and fortune of some professional athletes, Hollywood stars, and lottery winners. Their nervous systems can't handle the rushing torrent of abundance because they struggled in low energy vibration in the past. They burn through millions of dollars or, resort to drugs and alcohol. If you want to adopt a positive attitude and you're wondering why it's challenging, look at whom you hang out with and take inventory. Make a conscious decision to surround yourself with upbeat and clear-thinking individuals who are not in a rush to be noticed.

As you consider financial abundance and bringing more money into your life, look at the income of the top five people you hang around with, and their income will be about equal to your own. For some readers, that could be another reason to look for new friends. You don't need to focus on changing people; you need to focus on changing what you expect, and you will be surrounded by new people who fulfill your attitude for an abundant life. I am talking about the vibration, the energy, the set-point to give, and receive.

Additionally, how good of a friend are you to yourself? Do you ever give nice things to yourself as a reward? Do you say kind, encouraging words about yourself? You probably wouldn't have any friends at all if you said hurtful things to them. Do you say those same and hurtful things to yourself? If you do, know that you can treat yourself just as well as you treat those you find worthy of high respect. You might say, "Well it's the truth" or, "I'm just keepin' it real." But it is not the path to an abundant mindset.

Your mind is ready for wealth anytime you are set to the frequency of abundance. Metaphysically, you are in a state to truly receive after your mind is in check. Money follows your mindset.

After cleaning up my life and learning some basics about the 12 Steps, I came to realize I have no problem calling money to me. It happens with every venture I take on. I remember recently looking at a picture of a machine in a magazine, and I thought, "I could use another one of those." Five minutes later I talked to my machinist who came up to me with information about another business owner in Washington state who was offering exactly what I wanted in almost new condition for a deeply discounted price. I knew I deserved it and that it could happen without drama. This is my belief system thanks to working the 12 steps.

So how do you call in money for the first time? Start by getting rid of your emotional baggage so you can be in a happy state without lingering negativity. You can't just switch it on. You work diligently at first to guarantee success by being in a grateful state. The minute a thought of lack or negativity comes in, it can shut everything off. It will click off your power. Some people demand proof from Spirit. When it works, it's powerful, but when it doesn't, it can be a complete let down. Angry, demanding feelings often overpower everything else and don't work to bring you what you want. Switch on a grateful receiving mindset instead.

Pam Grout talks about her friend in her book who demanded proof from Spirit with gratitude. She said, "I need proof this is real. Within 48 hours I want someone to bring me a nice cool, green drink." Later that day she met with a friend, holding a green drink who said, "I thought you might like this." The key is to be in a high frequency with your thoughts. Negativity never serves you.

Another important part of having an abundant mindset is based on a good plan. If you're going to ask for money you have to understand what you intend to do with the money. When I started understanding abundance and manifesting, I was aware these magical things were happening in my life. But when I started truly grasping these concepts at a deeper level, things were popping into my life like popcorn everywhere.

I was almost in la-la-land, amazed at everything. I was at a stage where I demanded proof. "Prove to me this works," I'd call out. "I need evidence," I'd say. I was sort of working with it, checking out my own vibrational state. When I demanded it usually didn't work. When I came from gratitude and love, it almost always worked. Now I always manifest from a positive, high-vibrational state. I don't work with it consciously because it's become a part of my being. I believe it, so it doesn't take as much conscious effort as when I first started manifesting. A fast way to express what you want is with the phrase, "Be, do, and have." Another tip that works is believing it will be this – or something better. Then release it to the Universe and get into action. Remember to chill out. Some of the best gifts I've ever received from this process required no pushing at all.

ABUNDANCE IS NOT FORCED

I want to emphasize that you develop an "a conscious relationship" with your mind to manifest an attitude of abundance because it doesn't happen in an instant. Before the elevator ride with the salt and pepper shakers, I was clueless. I grew up with the idea you buckle down and work hard for everything before getting what you want. I had read so much about abundance, but it did not fit with my upbringing, so I couldn't accept it. I needed to see it illustrated. I came to understand that I had it backwards. The tough work and sheer, brute horsepower of hard labor shut the flow of abundance off. You may eventually get what you're striving for, but at a huge cost, that includes a lot of stress and sore muscles.

46

Instead of forcing, try affirming. Affirmations are short, powerful statements that help guide your thinking and actions. They generally begin with the words "I AM," and they affirm who you are and what you desire. Mostly, they get your thinking on track. Affirmations have become a natural part of my life because they never let me down. I have followed famous lines written by the sages, and I also have created my own.

One of my favorite affirmations I tell myself all the time is, "I AM always where I'm supposed to be when I'm supposed to be there." I'll walk around a corner, open a door, step into an office, or walk into my machine shop, and I'll be greeted by employees with a phone to his ear calling for my help. Other times I'll pick up my phone right when one of my daughters is calling. It's amazing how that little affirmation works. It always puts me in the place where I'm supposed to be at the ideal time. It's small, but it makes for less drama. And that keeps my mind free.

Another affirmation I use when I am looking for an answer: "It will be "*this*" or something better." I learned the phrase from my coach, Mary Morrissey. It is a reminder that the solution to whatever I'm dealing with might be right in front of me or something better is on the way. This particular affirmation helps me build trust in the Universe and keeps me from thinking obsessively about solutions.

The last affirmation I'll share is something I got from Dr. John D. Martini, "I AM a genius, and I listen to my wisdom." Don't laugh! You'll miss the magic if you do. This statement helps me get into the right mindset time and time again. I suggest that you try it; say it often and watch your mind open. It'll make an especially huge difference if you choose to adopt it into your everyday life.

I had to start creating my own affirmations and "mind tools" to avert my old idea of a constant push for something better. For me, affirmations get me out of the negative thoughts of lack. I have always thought of myself as a can-do thinker. But anytime I am not keyed in, acting from my true intentions, I am using my mind in the most limited way. I had to apply the principle of positive thinking to be fully on board, and that's when the real power of the universe multiplied my results exponentially.

THE HAPPY VIBE

I earned enough money to support myself and family, but when people asked if I was happy, the answer was almost always, "No." Back in my early adult years, I was dissatisfied with pretty much everything. I was striving and fighting which goes counter to abundance thinking. Instead of letting anything flow toward me, I always scrapped my way through and provided the basics. That's the American way, right? Work harder to get results even when they could be better. The problem was I didn't have much direction. When I look back, I can see that drugs provided an element of escapism so I didn't have to feel lost. But I was constantly bothered by the thought there was something more waiting for me. If you're thinking about what you don't have, that's exactly what you get more of -- NOTHING. Conversely, if you're focused on what's positive, then you'll attract more of what you enjoy. I came to understand that's how the Law of Abundance works. And that was a huge motivator to help me pay attention to my thoughts. Which ideas were sabotaging me and which ones held me accountable?

When I first learned about affirmations I was skeptical. However, other former skeptics suggested, "Go ahead and at least give it a shot." Within a short time, I noticed I was getting positive results from my affirmations as things I thought about suddenly started coming into my reality. I now believe positive affirmations have the ability to increase your energy to a higher vibration, and as a result, attract what you're thinking about.

RECOGNIZING INTEGRITY IN OTHERS

I have three people working for me who are convicted felons, and they're hard-working, reliable employees. Many business owners won't take a chance hiring a person with a prison record. One had been a mechanic for eight years. It takes the belief that a person who has been to prison has both possibility and potential. He's a highly capable mechanic, but the idea of considering a bright future was whipped out of him while being institutionalized. He's gradually coming around and accepting more responsibility. I was like that to a certain extent when I left the Marines. Some educational systems do that to people as well. I was told to think a certain way, but it's not always beneficial because it might not produce the best version of "self." No longer am I a person who stays inside the box or colors inside the lines.

I understand I'll make mistakes, we all do. But when it happens, I think it is important to acknowledge a mistake, take responsibility, and solve the problem. That's a person high in integrity, who's forward-thinking and able to step out of their comfort zone. There are constant growth and learning curves that never end throughout your life; however, it gets easier with practice. You can tell the people who have worked on it by how they show up in the world and how much control they have over their thoughts.

LIVE BY YOUR VALUES

Being truthful with yourself makes it easier. When your actions are in alignment with your core values, you live in truth and express it daily. Doing this requires an awareness of your personal core values. Understanding your core values only happens through patient self-exploration. Go ahead and make a list. It's up to you whether it's on paper, a smartphone app, and or your tablet or your laptop. Success means different things to different people. Ask yourself this question: What's important about success to me?

Make your list of things that spell success to you. These are your general values. Remember, it's not about what your parents think or what your friends think; it's what YOU think that matters. Here are a few examples of what success means to some people:

- Making as much money as possible?
- Owning a business?
- Being a well-known author?
- Creative expression through painting or other art forms?
- Having close personal ties with friends and family?
- Raising great kids to have what you didn't have?
- Traveling the world and studying other cultures?
- Getting an education that includes advanced degrees?
- Being super healthy and fit?

Perhaps a balanced blend of some of these success factors appeals to you, as you certainly don't have to choose just one. This short list is to get your wheels turning. What matters most is where you're at right now. Are you aligning your actions to get more of what you want? Ask yourself, "Do I agree with things I didn't actually agree to?"

Did you grow up where certain ideas and norms were forced upon you? You've seen this happen on social media when friends "go along" to avoid being judged. But when you determine what's important to you and act in alignment with your values, not only are you able to express your brilliance, creativity, and truth, but you also develop your highest opportunity to be successful. For years, I was told that I was a "natural" when it came to putting something together. Plus, I enjoyed solving things. The combination of working with my hands and thinking through a puzzle made me happy. When I realized this, I felt tuned into my purpose, and my mission seemed clear. I knew I would one day have the shop I dreamed about.

THE SHADOW SIDE OF ABUNDANCE

When you think about that which you lack, your subconscious doesn't know the difference between "having" and "not having." Sometimes it is easy to notice all that another person has and you might find yourself asking, "Why don't I have it yet?" It's very important to keep your attention on all you have and all you are creating. You never want to impose limits by focusing on a situation you believe is lacking in the present moment. Our subconscious mind doesn't know the difference between not having and having. When we say we don't have something, the subconscious mind doesn't take it as good or bad. It just perceives "this is the truth." So, part of your subconscious is the transmitter which receives input and downloads from Spirit. Turn the transmitter on, increase your vibration, and you'll get more of whatever is your most dominant thought.

In the 2006 documentary, *"What the Bleep Do We Know?"* scientists explain the more you have a particular thought pattern about something over and over again, the more imprinted it becomes in your mind. Over time, the patterns become deeply etched into your neuro-transmitters. When you make a conscious decision to begin changing a particular thought pattern, the longer you've been thinking those thoughts, the more effort it takes to create new neuro-pathways.

I like to think of it this way: Just because the engineer hits the "stop" button on a train doesn't mean the train will stop that very moment. It might slow down over a stretch of ten miles before coming to a complete stop. When the engines are turned on again, it takes several miles to gather momentum and get the train back up to full speed. As much as possible, you want to align your thoughts with possibilities, not circumstances that you find lacking.

Some of these practices take time and patience to become a new habit, so you stop doing what you don't want to do. While you're trying to change your thoughts, any negative self-talk will cancel out everything. While in the process of changing your thoughts, it's almost like the movie "Groundhog Day" starring Bill Murray from 1993. The practice is to repeat the new thoughts over and over again to create a new and better habit ingrained in the subconscious mind until the new thought pattern is the dominant one. Once it happens, everyday outcomes start clicking into place and life feels easy, even magical.

DISSOLVING NEGATIVE THOUGHTS

You have probably noticed, too, with the rise of social media and instant fame, more and more ordinary people present news ideas as though it is truth. In the past, journalists were required to verify all facts in an article before publishing. There was a system of checks and balances before going to print. If you buy into negative, exaggerated headlines and believe they're true, you'll lower your energy and begin thinking negative thoughts.

People dedicated to remaining in a high vibration reduce what they watch on television or news unless it comes from a trusted news source. They've removed his sort of negativity out of their reality, and it works for them.

At some point, you still should be informed to make worthwhile decisions. However, choosing where you set your attention and whom you allow into your space – even if it's just a talking head – will have an impact on your energy. You won't flow with good vibrations if your abundance of energy is wasted.

No one knows more about dissolving negativity than the late Wayne Dyer. He was a master of setting intentions, and he had a following of several hundreds of thousands of people in the US alone who sent his book, *The Power of Intention,* to #1 on the New Your Times list within four days after its release. He was a man deeply inspired by the power of the mind. Dr. Dyer paid attention to idiosyncrasies occurring in nature and used them as his "classroom" to master the questions he pondered. I recall how he fictionalized his observations to get his followers laughing.

In one of his lectures, he told a story about a cat who was looking for happiness. Everywhere he went, other cats told him happiness was located in the tip of his tail. He didn't believe it at first, but other cats confirmed the same thing, "Yes, happiness is in the tip of every cat's tail." So, he chased his tail. Round and round and round he went in circles until he got exhausted. Then he learned from the wisest old cat if he just walked around proudly, happiness would follow him wherever he went.

If you're open to receiving what you want, or if you're open to receiving something even better, you will set your mind to be aligned with your Higher Power. This is the nature of abundance. We establish dreams, visions, goals, and transmit that information through prayer. In reply, your Source of greatest good will start sending opportunities your way. The tricky part is not controlling how, when, or in what capacity it will all take place. Sometimes you will receive only a portion of what you said you wanted. Soon you'll notice more is manifesting because you did not give into negative thinking.

RELEASE AND DETACH

Detachment isn't so much about not attaching yourself to the outcome you want but attaching yourself more to your journey, a feeling of breaking through, and an openness to anything that might lie ahead along your path. I know people who plan every single detail of their day at home, and especially when they travel. I know others who fly to a foreign country and have a room reserved for the first couple days, a car rented for convenience, and a loose agenda, keeping them open to whatever they discover. Who do you think has a better time? Wherever I'm supposed to be I know I'll be there and everything will be fine. I'm completely detached from the idea I have to plan out every hour whether at work or play. That way, I'm open to the day unfolding in whatever way is perfect.

At first, it was difficult to detach from wanting certain results, but it didn't take too long to figure out that being open to new, undiscovered possibilities gave me a sense of accomplishment and personal freedom. As a man's man. I always wanted to be totally in control. I wasn't a big planner, but I knew the outcome I wanted. If an event didn't occur the way I wanted, I found it extremely stressful and upsetting because I was so attached to the results that I thought were best. A big part of detachment is letting go of the outcomes you feel are best and accept that life is a journey.

Another part of detaching is the realization we aren't in control. A friend of mine told me it was a big lesson for her to learn to say, "I don't know." She always felt she had to come up with a good answer if someone asked her a question. If she came up with an answer, she felt pressured it better be the right one. To reach the point where she could say "I don't know, but I intend to figure it out" took effort. When she started doing it, she felt more empowered because she wasn't rushed and she had the faith the answer would come to her.
By saying "I don't know," she wasn't responsible for the outcome.

THIS OR SOMETHING EVEN BETTER

When you choose to state a goal or intention, always say, "I want this or something better." By doing so, you create an open space to receive your goal or something better. Additionally, you are detaching from what may be limited thinking at the moment. Allow for the opportunity to break through and be open to receiving something better.

Saying "I want" helps you practice detachment as well. Removing the words, "I need" eliminates a sense of powerlessness and neediness. Replace it with the words, "I want" instead. You attach too much to the outcome when you say, "I need." A statement such as, "I need the perfect partner, or I won't be happy." That's attaching a lot of emotional baggage to your request. When you say, "I want to do x" rather than "I need to do x," you're more detached from an emotional expectation. Next time you catch yourself saying "I need" cancel that thought and replace it with "I want" so you're less emotionally attached to a specific outcome.

Learn to practice and trust the process of detaching. When you move in the direction of getting into a mindset of detachment, the magic happens quickly, and you'll see the power in detaching. Sometimes we have blinders on and don't know that there could be something better, which is why it can be challenging at first. If you don't see something better at the moment, it means to be open for something you can't see yet. This is an important key and requires your faith in the matter. Tell yourself, "I am excited to see what happens or where this is going."

When you're open, miracles begin taking shape. An attitude of abundance is always rewarded by "this" intention you have set, or something even better. It's a spiritual law of the universe.

MY STORY:

PART 2

"You cannot run around changing the world when you are too afraid to make changes within yourself."

~Alan Cohen, Hay House author of
The Dragon Doesn't Live Here Anymore

I really thought I had everything in place. At age 41, I understood the keys and I was practicing them. I was out of bed early every morning and drove straight to the shop. On the outside, my life looked good – job, wife, kids, employees – but I had no one to rely on outside of myself when things got really tough. I took away the alcohol, but I still had a few great ideas to try out, such as sneaking weed back into my life.

Abstaining from all substance is the key to sobriety. People like me can get cocky and fool themselves into thinking that there's no harm in a little treat from time to time. I tried hard to live a double life – pretend I was completely sober – and that's when it all came crashing down. I really had not established a regime of surrender.

It shouldn't have to take hitting rock bottom to finally wake up and connect with Spirit each day, but that's what had to happen for me. I love the quote, "Religion is for people afraid to go to Hell and spirituality is for people who've already been there." On November 10th, 2003, I made a very important decision to leave my version of a living hell.

Remember, I grew up with no conscious awareness of emotional connection. I was a tough, hard-working, hard-drinking man's man, raised in a non-practicing, Presbyterian family. Religious education wasn't a part of my life that mattered or had much impact on my thoughts or ideas. I believed in the idea there was a God out in the cosmos somewhere, the creator of all things. But I felt no conscious connection to that belief. Most people have an inherent ability to think about God based on their experiences because it's part of our society and culture. Even our money says, "In God We Trust." However, I had a "coming to Jesus" transforming of endless gratitude and abundance after my third round of alcohol treatment.

For better or worse, I had to reach a point of desperation where I was literally on my knees. Typically, people come to understand spirituality through their own rock bottom moments. It doesn't have to be that way, but for a lot of people that's how they arrive at the point where they say, "Okay, I'm willing to accept a Higher Power into my life."

In the earlier days of AA, I had seen people operating from an incredible place of faith and understanding about themselves and a greater force "out there." I had seen synchronicities at work, but I was not one-hundred percent certain *it could happen to me*, too. And that's why I hit rock bottom:

I was separated from my wife. I couldn't see my kids. I was losing my business. And on a minute by minute basis, I felt totally out of control. My mind had so much power over me. I was losing it all so fast! Surprisingly, the moments when I felt most in control were when I got high or drunk. I reached a point where I couldn't smoke enough marijuana fast enough to get the feeling I wanted. I was literally burning the back of my throat due to smoking so much weed. On top of that, I'd drink so much so fast my body was drunk, but my mind was still sharp, racing with thoughts. I couldn't drink anymore, I couldn't even walk, but I couldn't shut my mind off, either. It was still clipping along at two-hundred miles an hour.

An incessant monkey chatter was ricocheting around in my head. It never stopped, and it was always negative. Monkey chatter says things like:

- "You can't do THAT!"
- "Who do you think you ARE!"
- "You're a failure."
- "Why can't you get your act together?"
- "What a PHONY!"

It seemed impossible to be happy and live a successful life. How was I to meet my goals and dreams with constant nattering nabobs of negativity bouncing around in my head?

My business was growing so fast. It was growing outside its boundaries in a way I couldn't control. Smoking and drinking were my way of coping. My marriage was falling apart, and I had an affair. I was going insane. I was doing every dumb thing you could possibly imagine because I just got too big for my britches.

I didn't understand all the things I agreed to unconsciously, and I had lost track of how long it had been going on. According to me, I was a tough guy, and the world revolved around me. I had no ability to track all my stinking-thinking and manipulation. I was masterful at organizing situations so that results favored me. My every idea focused around, *What can I get? What's in this for me?* Most of all, God was just something "out there," as I had no way to relate to the Higher Power that I had heard about in the rooms of AA. My ego was in charge, and I was a huge false persona growing out of control.

I remember lying in the back of my truck so drunk I couldn't move. I couldn't even lift my arm. My mind was still racing, crisp with thoughts and chatter. In fact, it was crackling with so much incessant chatter it didn't seem like I was drunk. I desperately wanted to shut it down, heal the pain, and feel good again. But then I'd recover the next day and go back to the shop!

Every day I'd say, "This is it. I have to stop today." The next day I'd go back to my shop and work a full day. Even though I'd start the day hung over, I could function. Or at least I thought I was functioning. Four o'clock would roll around, and I'd say, "I can do it again. It's okay, I can handle it," and I'd start drinking all over again. I could rationalize any irrational behavior. I had no way to shut off all the never-ending thoughts bouncing around like steel pinballs flinging around in my mind. I also didn't have a system to trust and have faith in all the good things happening at the same time. I had no Higher Power to trust, and I could not believe this mess of my life would ever turn around. I mistakenly thought I was the one with the power who had to stay on top of everything. Like so many people in AA, I had to be brought to my knees. This time, I had absolutely nothing left.

For a third time, I was headed towards intensive rehabilitation at an inpatient facility. Not exactly a hospital, but pretty similar – they called it a "center." I told my shop assistant, "If I disappear, it is because I'm headed for the center." One day I decided it was time. I got my mom to drive me there along with my uncle. Next, I called my accountant, but he didn't get it. He asked, "How can you take a sabbatical for 30 days when you have so much going on?" I replied, "Dude if I don't go now, there'll be nothing left of me or my business. It's better for everyone that I'm gone for 21 days and then salvage what I can."

TREATMENT: ROUND THREE

Years earlier, I had read a book on a flight to Alaska, remember? Well, I carried that into the doors of treatment with me. It was the only personal growth book to which I paid any attention. I'm sure you've heard the expression, "When the student is ready, the teacher appears." I read the book in treatment with a new sense of curiosity. I literally was not able to fight or apply any force; I had to surrender to a new way of thinking. This time, I truly wanted it.

I watched a documentary outlining the medical reasons people become addicted and how it works scientifically. They were describing this thing in our brains like little Pac-Man characters chewing and eating brain cells. Everything clicked. I had to come this far to embrace the idea "I am a powerless over alcohol" as the first Step of AA proclaims. The journaling I did in treatment helped me realize the necessity to make that shift. I'd share my story and then others would share their story. I began seeing I was powerless over the chemicals I took in for so long. The next step was believing there was a power greater than myself. That's the Higher Power whom I thought I knew from AA literature, but not really. So far, I had resisted giving away my own will so that this power could take charge.

I promised to attend 90 meetings in 90 days. I found a sponsor, and he said, "Believe that I believe until you can see it works and you'll believe it for yourself." Still looking for more proof and guidance, I came across an article in Reader's Digest claiming medical evidence how working the Twelve Steps changes the brain. All 12 steps of AA focus on your attitude and thinking. That's the moment a light bulb went off because now there was medical evidence proving our brains physically change when we make the commitment to connect with Spirit. I had to trust the process. I had a sense that my dedication would determine whether I made it or not. There was absolutely no way I wanted to go to re-hab again.

No alcoholic can understand that trying to make the self-happy with external substances will always lead to a dead end. The addicted mind pushes on for the next great answer. For many of us, we run out of answers. I spent 21 days in intensive inpatient treatment and detoxing was one of the roughest experiences I have ever endured. There are night sweats and a total inability to sleep. I experienced brain flashes because fat cells store THC, the active ingredient in marijuana. I thought this might never end.

But the great news is that you are cared for and you can't go home and it does end, eventually. Finally, a working mind! *No more days of spinning in thoughts and fear.* I had enough, and I was ready to change! It was like coming out of the darkness and into the bright sunshine of possibilities.

If you have never had to say goodbye to your life as you knew it, my adventures in rehab may sound far-fetched. Yet, anyone who has been through it and really wanted the magic knows what I'm talking about. It took a deep surrender to understanding that there is a Higher Power that I can plug into that gives me complete guidance with ease. When I plug in, I understand that the sheer horsepower I need does not come from me. My sponsor said, "Believe that *I believe* in a Higher Power until you can believe in a Higher Power. Watch me until you believe." I could see that some people in AA were living extraordinary lives. They'd tell me, "You might want to look at what you're thinking about."

Since treatment, I've had a love affair with gaining knowledge and wisdom. I've read countless books, listened to audios, attended seminars and workshops and applied the wisdom as much as possible to my life. Mary's congregation met in Bellevue, Washington and I frequented those events along with more responsibility to my local AA community.

SPIRIT METAPHOR: THE KIRBY VACUUM CLEANER

There's a company that makes vacuum cleaners named Kirby Vacuums. They were famous back in the day, and they're still manufactured in Cleveland Ohio. Kirby's are built like a tank with thick, stainless steel housing. Ask your mom or grandma about it. A Kirby can suck a golf ball through a garden hose, even a 50-year-old one. They're self-powered, and when you plug one in and turn it on, it'll go anywhere. You almost have to steer it and hang on for the ride. They move effortlessly and have boundless energy and power when they're switched on.

BUT...when the power is turned off, it becomes heavy, cumbersome and a struggle to push or steer, even for just a few feet. That's a good example of what it's like being unplugged from Spirit, God, Your Source or "the Force." When your connection is strong, life hums along happily almost on automatic pilot. Understanding who you are and how amazing you are is important to growing and learning to love yourself. Good things start happening almost effortlessly. Without that connection, everything feels like hard, hard work.

I saw this exact connection to Spirit working in other people's lives and said, "I've got to try it. I have nothing else left." But you don't have to reach the extreme low I reached to start enjoying a better life, more joy, more prosperity, and more everything. I would hear other guys in AA say, "How badly do you want it?" Finally, I could see with new eyes. My over-developed ego prevented God from enriching my life. I was used to being in charge. My ego made all my plans. In fact, some people say "ego" means "Edging God Out." When I started grasping that concept, it was like putting a throttle on my ego. I no longer worked for my ego; it worked for me. I surrendered my ego to Higher Power and my "Kirby Vacuum" flowed effortlessly.

I learned from Mary's book that the ego lives in the past or the future. There's no way for it to live in the now, this present moment. Ego worries about the past and frets about the future. It ponders over senseless thoughts, such as, "How can I impress this person?" Or, "Why did I do that?" Those thoughts cannot survive in the present. Basically, the ego is powerless anytime I am fully present, but I had to get out of my regular surroundings to really experience the magic.

Connecting with nature is an awesome way to enjoy the beauty and power of Spirit at work. Rivers, lakes, trees, beaches, and even a backyard garden are representations of natural beauty. All are Spirit in action because they're created and powered from it. Connecting can be as simple as sitting in a forest, on a beach or even in a pretty park and quietly paying attention to what's around you. I followed the ideas of Dr. Wayne Dyer from his book *Getting in the Gap* where he talks about, "the space between the notes." By sitting in nature, especially around old red rocks and canyons, I felt a "oneness" with peace and silence. My mind welcomed the sounds of nature as a place to call home.

Over time, more dreams would manifest in ways I could not have predicted. My voice was always commented on – people could not help but remark that my voice is deep and stands out. I needed time in a sober program and the guidance of Mary Morrissey's teachings to get in touch with my calling. My dream was clear: I wanted to use my voice to make an impact.

I want to share with you five questions that helped me every day as I got centered in my new life as a man committed to my success and recovery. These questions helped me build my dreams for my hydraulic business, radio show, and speaking platform. These questions also kept me connected each and every day to the present moment and my purpose. I would think about the radio show or my work in Toastmasters and ask:

- Does it give me more life?
- Does it align with my core values?
- Does it make me grow?
- Does it require help from a higher power?
- Does it have good in it for others?

Suddenly more doors opened as I launched my spirituality radio show and became a member of 7 local speech clubs through Toastmasters International. Remember, I was just a farm hard from Nebraska. I had no idea the gifts that would result from admitting I was powerless over alcohol and finding my way into one new growth opportunity after another. Pretty soon, 300,000 people were in my circle.

LIFE MASTERY KEY

#4

HEALTH

"Follow what most excites you and the right people,

the right materials, and the right opportunities will show up."

~Pam Grout, the author of

Thank and Grow Rich: A 30 Day Experiment

In Shameless Gratitude and Unabashed Joy

Of course, our health is about our physical bodies, but being concerned and understanding the metaphysical principle of your health is mostly about mindset, not physique. Yet it is safe to say that your body cannot thrive if you are carrying emotional clutter, neglecting sleep, thinking crazy thoughts, and letting others control your life. Do you have practices set up to relieve stress, such as prayer or meditation? Is there anyone you follow on a weekly basis who helps you re-set your goals or holds you accountable for your future plans? Attending to any of this ensures stronger health and over all well-being. Spiritual teacher Caroline Myss once said at a public forum, "People can survive a great amount of time on just cat food if they have their emotional and spiritual health intact."

In order for me to stick with a sober program, I had to commit to abstaining from alcohol completely, all the time, no matter what. By doing so, I proclaim my commitment to a balanced life of physical, spiritual, and emotional health. After three visits to the treatment center, I did not want to fail ever again. But I noticed that some people in the program had something that I was seriously struggling with. They had a relationship to a higher power and a commitment to living a spiritual life. I found myself curious since the people who were spiritually attentive appeared healthy. It seemed that their mind was "fit."

I'll be one hundred percent honest with you because that's my nature. I had a big problem dedicating myself and my personal growth to, "The God Thing." Because I am not loyal to one teaching, nor a member of an organized faith, I now call my understanding of spirituality "the Spirit thing." It took time getting familiar with terms in the AA literature, but now I feel comfortable using terms such as: Spirit, Source, and Higher Power. But I didn't always.

While addicted to alcohol and marijuana, I was finally DONE in 2003. I hit rock bottom, as this seemed to be the only way my stubborn ego finally got in touch with who was on the inside. Who was Todd, anyway? I was such a tough guy and I had practiced turning off my true voice and truest feelings for all my life. I did not know my real self. The idea that I had a peaceful side to me completely eluded all my thoughts. I was most familiar with my demons and aware they were ruling my life; however, I still wanted to think I had *some* control, even if only by hanging on with my fingertips. AA literature adds "powerless" to the very first step. After working so hard to be independent, it was difficult to fathom the idea I was powerless and that "God" was watching out for me.

Being open to accepting support and guidance requires humility. For you, it may not require hitting your own version of rock bottom. In fact, I hope that never happens! But that's what it took for me. My sponsor was a great guide who told me, "It's about whatever you can grasp to start." Knowing that I was a mechanic, he'd combine practical ideas with spiritual ones, "There's a power greater than you in the Universe even if that power is something as clear cut as the electricity running through your house." That I could swallow! Still, I was looking for a concrete sign. Even as low as I fell, I still wanted proof.

I was attending AA meetings two, three, and four times a week. I kept asking for a sign that would give me positive proof I was doing the right thing. One day in deep despair, I asked for a sign to be revealed…today! I went to a meeting and met a guy I'd never seen before. His first name was also Todd. We struck up a conversation. He was a personable, outgoing guy and I enjoyed his positive energy.

He asked me, "Do you know the meaning of our name?" That seemed like a weird question, and then he said, "Todd means fox." I thought about a children's cartoon my daughters watched called, "The Fox and the Hound" and the little fox cartoon character was named Todd. I don't remember much more about our conversation because I was still obsessing about my need for a sign – I was eager to see or know that Spirit was looking out for me.

I got in my truck and was driving down Grand Avenue. At the time, this street was very significant in my life; the meeting was held in a center on Grand Avenue. My apartment was on Grand Avenue, and just a few blocks beyond was my machine shop, also on Grand Avenue. My whole world was centered on one street and I drove up and down it numerous times every day.

I was now one block away from the meeting hall and driving toward my apartment. I looked to the right, and there was a red fox. You could say he was jogging on the sidewalk and keeping pace with my truck. I went extra slow, watching him more than I watched the road. This went on for about ten blocks until I reached a stoplight near my shop. My apartment was 50 yards further down the street. I stopped at the light and watched the fox in complete awe. Right before my shop was an alley. He turned, blew down the alley and disappeared. I had lived in Everett Washington for 40 years and never seen a fox.

I know, crazy, right? So, there was my sign! You could have hit me upside the head with a brick; I was stunned. It was truly moving for me and it changed my outlook on the idea of Spirit. I felt accepting and ready for Spirit to enter my heart. It happened that fast. I was hooked on a power larger than myself, and it was exactly what I needed to improve the health of my mindset.

If you were raised with a spiritual belief system but grew disinterested, do not think there is something wrong with you. I encourage you to believe in something – perhaps the mysteries of nature -- until you get your own sign you are doing the right thing. You don't have to believe in my fox story. If you're paying attention, you'll get your sign, and you will see your own "fox."

A common idea is that others have Spirit guiding them, but there was not enough to go around for all of us. I promise, if your eyes are open, you will see your sign. As you start to believe even more in yourself, the signs will show up, and your doubts will die off. Those signs will help you accept whatever concept of a spirit guide shows up in your life offering love and support. It is a Source consistently providing ease and direction. I don't think there would be so much emphasis on the significance of Source for thousands of years if there weren't something incredibly important about it.

To build a relationship with a power greater than "the self" is a way to care for our well-being and promote our health. You have experienced synchronicity over and over at different points in your life, right? It's a part of being human although many naysayers simply explain it away as "just a coincidence." Are you paying attention when synchronicities occur? If so, you may wonder:

- How did this happen?
- Where did this money / job / friend come from?
- How did that person know to show up?
- Why did a fox run alongside my truck for ten blocks?

We think there must be a logical solution, a concrete answer or understanding to everything. You'll find this out in your own way, but logic is highly over-rated. These occurrences are beyond our understanding because we live in a miraculous universe where some events seem unexplainable. Nonetheless, they're so real. Opening up to Spirit, a power so much greater than myself, was the game-changer I needed to stay sober. Until then, I always knew it was up to me, and I worried what would happen as soon as I was tapped out.

MEDITATION

I strongly suggest you start meditating. You won't notice a big difference right off the bat, but you'll notice tiny changes that start adding up in a big way. This is how meditation began for me. I wondered at first if I was just wasting my time, but now I have a routine and so many benefits! There are so many styles and experts who can lead you through the process. I am not a meditation teacher, but I know that I am free of a deep mental grooves of monkey chatter thanks to meditation. The same freedom can be yours.

I also encourage you to use your meditation as a spring board for advancing your visions and manifesting goals. Once you've been doing meditation daily for about a month, sit down and write out your goals. It can be a short-term goal, something you want to accomplish in the next 60 days or something you want to achieve in the next year. Remember to write things in terms of what you DO want, not what you don't want.

Here is a process that has created big shifts for me. Instead of writing, "I want to feel less stressed" I will write, "I feel calm and peaceful." Instead of, "I'm tired of being broke" write, "I'll have an additional $10,000 this year." Next, choose a thought and use it as a mantra when you meditate. With each breath say, "Calm… calm… calm…" watch how you'll gradually start feeling more calm and peaceful. Or say, "$10,000 more, $10,000 more…" and watch the money-making ideas that germinate and grow in your mind. I know people who've used this technique, and they've all reported it's like a super charger for their goals and dreams. And not in a manic, stressed out way, but in a calm, happy, "I've got this" kind of way. Do this on a daily basis, and after a short time, you'll feel happier, more confident and more aligned with your purpose.

GETTING INTO THE FLOW AND LEADING BY EXAMPLE

Once I knew I had the power to stop the ramblings of my incessant thinking, my mind was no longer like a Super Ball thrown in a closet with the door slammed shut. I actively studied how to retrain and re-program my brain. In geek terminology, I was rebooting a new operating system. Consciously, I knew I was redoing my life and my thoughts. Not only was I in synch meditating and honoring my goals, but I saw how other people in my 12-step program believed and operated. I came to believe if things are possible for them, then things are possible for me.

I finally saw happy people who didn't drink. Until then, I didn't know what that was like. I didn't know I could feel normal without being inebriated. As a sober person, I felt peaceful, prosperous, and happy. The old timers had to believe it first, and then I followed. I understood this was the right path for me because everything else I tried simply had not worked. I asked for guidance from Spirit, listened to my sponsor, and developed trust in my intuition. It felt like true magic unfolding.

Recognizing the ability and power to choose my thoughts was a revelation. With every door I opened, every stoplight I paused at, every turn I made in life, everything brought me to this point right here and right now. I was living intentionally and manifesting my own reality. So many people get caught up worrying about being ridiculed and criticized. When we are committed to a great level of health and well-being, we train our minds to focus and create the next chapter of our lives without lingering distractions. Each person we partner with or build our plans with has had some, if not many experiences at failure, embarrassment, exhaustion, and poor decision-making. They've also known great experiences full of satisfaction, success, and confidence. We need not take any of it personally. That was a huge gift I got from meditating and honoring my own well-being.

For the first few years I owned my business, I struggled with being a business owner, having compassion, and realizing when customers and employees were calling out for love. I could be a real jerk. My Dad was a nice guy, but he also was a big jerk when it came to business and managing people. His behaviors influenced mine because I thought if my Dad does it then it must be right. As I learned to be more compassionate, more sides of my personality emerged. I found my feminine side and started buying flowers for my office. I got one ear pierced. I went to a mentor and asked her, "Isn't all this compassion and kindness stuff in conflict with being a business owner, a boss and managing people?"

She looked at me and said, "You still have to be the boss." It hit me, and I understood she was saying you still have to be firm, but you can do it with compassion. Then I got involved with Toastmasters International, an organization whose purpose is helping people gain leadership and public speaking skills. I discovered you could give creative, constructive criticism in a kind way without making people wrong. My old ways have changed from being the boss with harsh criticism and words like, "I can't believe you did that." "What were you thinking?" I degraded them and let them know mistakes were dumb, and so were they. Now I look for teachable moments sandwiched in between compliments.

The way I show up today is a major contrast to some of the examples I had as a kid. For my kids, I've done my best to model by example and conduct my life with conscious manifesting instead of knee-jerk reactions. This is part of my metaphysical health and commitment to being present in my day to day life.

You might have a gentler style already. Perhaps you are not from a rural or blue-collar background. I am very accustomed to hearing people spout off whatever is on their mind. It was just part of my upbringing. Even the person with the "A-list" of degrees could use a lesson in manifesting dreams. After all, the key to great results begins with a solid mindset and the belief that your every dream is in the hands of your highest Source.

HAPPINESS IS A HEALTHY CHOICE

I started this chapter with a quote from a very inspirational author. Pam Grout is a travel writer who is really in the groove especially since she found *A Course in Miracles* and has applied her own spin to start the day right. She is the writer of E-Squared and E-Cubed, both filled with fun exercises to improve your mindset by journeying through heart-felt silliness. I love her style, which poured over to the pages of *Thank and Grow Rich*, her latest book, and one that plays with the splendid title of Napoleon Hill's classic, *Think and Grow Rich*.

While thumbing through the pages, I found this fun exercise. Anytime I need to freshen up my internal dialogue or get my head in a good space; I look for easy exercises or affirmations to set me straight. I love this one:

Party Game #1: AA 2.0

My name is Pam Grout, and I am a joy and happiness freak. To celebrate, I launched a brand-new chapter of AA. Unlike version 1.0, my AA stands for "Amazing Awesomeness," and it only has two steps.

Step #1: Admit that "something amazingly awesome is going to happen" to you today. First thing every morning, before you throw off the covers, before you leap out of bed, before you fire up the old Mr. Coffee, proclaim to the world that something unexpected, exciting, and **amazingly awesome** *is headed your way today.*

It takes, what, three, four seconds? Yet it's one of the most important things you can do each morning. The first few minutes of every day pre-paves the next 24 hours with positive expectations. It sets up a powerful intention, a forecast on which you now choose to focus. And it never fails to come true.

Step 2: Come to believe…in blessings and miracles. Pretend to be a private investigator assigned the task of finding all the beauty and largesse in the world. The dominant paradigm might suggest otherwise but practiced with regularity; this ritual will allow you to see things in a whole different light. Instead of looking for problems, be on the hunt for blessings. You'll find, to paraphrase the description of the old radio character Chichenman, "They're everywhere. They're everywhere."

To make sure your thoughts don't return to their slacking tendencies, text (or tweet or post them on Instagram) three blessings (aka amazing awesomeness) each morning. The only stipulation is the items on your list must be different each day.

What are you doing each day to enliven your mood and set yourself up for a healthy, limitless, and open mindset? It is healthy to stop for water, smell the roses, get out in nature, and tend to your diet, but very little of that matters if you walk through life with a mind that plots against you. Dedicate yourself to the flow of a brave new and awakened mind and start each day, one foot in front of the other, with an attitude for great success.

Life Mastery Key

#5

Love

"You must unlearn what you have learned."

~Yoda, Jedi Master

Many of us have been conditioned to focus mostly on romantic love. And understandably so – it feels good to be loved by one special person. But the key to being in love and sustaining love comes from a deep acceptance of self, of others, and of everyone. We were not meant to only love one person and bicker with everyone else. The key to great love is to be open and accepting.

It may be hard to hear, but if you can't accept others, you are not operating from a place of love. You cannot truly know the experience of love without the experience of acceptance. It is crucial to understand that acceptance is not agreeing to something false or condoning a ridiculous idea. Acceptance is an understanding that something merely is so. It is an admittance to fact. "She says she wants to fly to the moon." The act of acceptance understands her desire to fly to the moon is so. It doesn't matter if you think she'll make it or not.

"The first step toward change is awareness. The second step is acceptance."
--Nathaniel Branden,

ACCEPTANCE PRECEDES LOVE

In my experience, acceptance has not come naturally. It's a mind-bender. You'll need to practice allowing your mind to observe how it works. Even though the agreement is not the equivalent of accepting another person, we do it all the time, usually to keep a false sense of peace. You are often in a natural form of agreement with people you choose to hang out with the most or when good luck comes your way.

When your friend likes your ideas, and complements you, the agreement is easy and obvious.

But what about when you feel out of alignment with another person? What then? Do you avoid your friend? Some people find it very useful and justify the thought...*I'll just avoid my friend because he said something I can't agree with. We just won't hang out for a while.* It is important to stop and see how you show up with others if they are not in agreement with your ideas. By having this awareness, you can stop avoiding friends and take the challenge to be accepting of what is so. We all have the right to our own thoughts and ideas.

I used to feel very uncomfortable when someone did not agree with me, and I would instantly find something else to do, or I'd change the subject. I had no concept that it was fine to work for people or make friends with people who were not in complete agreement with my ideas. Like everything else we've been talking about, I had to get uncomfortable before I found a new way to show up and stand firmly in my own ideas.

I learned that being in agreement with everyone is not the key to a good life. *Acceptance,* not agreement, is the key to understanding love. And, acceptance is a choice.

Think of acceptance as something similar to water. Never does water flow uphill. You can't "will" the flow of water to turn a corner if it has the option to flow straight down. Water is always on the path of least resistance. I believe acceptance of new ideas is just like the flow of water. When you accept something or someone, you are really on the simplest path toward personal abundance and love. Remember, I am not talking about standing behind an idea that doesn't mesh with your understanding. Acceptance may or may not include an agreement with others. When you accept an idea, you realize this is how it is for your life, your career, for another person, a group of people, even a nation. This is so. You accept that fact even if you don't agree with it.

What are some things you can accept even if you don't like it?

- I accept that I got a ticket for parking in a loading zone.
- I accept that my sister cannot visit for the holidays.
- I accept that my boss has left me in charge for the upcoming week.
- I accept that I have to manage my grandmother's estate.

Acceptance is counterintuitive because it requires you to open your mind and remove judgment, fear, and doubt regarding some situation or person. It might seem like this has nothing to do with love, but the opposite of love is fear. A sense of love cannot be present where fear and judgment reign. Acceptance is necessary if you intend to get to love. See what happens if you choose not to accept:

I cannot accept that my sister is not coming for the holidays.
I cannot accept that the dishes were not done
I cannot accept that my boss won't promote me

86

As Doctor Phil might say, how's that working for you? Do you have any forward motion when you refuse to accept what is? Do you experience a sense of love? Absolutely not.

When your best friend suddenly packs up and moves across the country, you might not feel loved regarding their decision until you accept the circumstances. Perhaps your friend has been offered a great opportunity. Similarly, when your boss tells you that layoffs will affect 10% of the company, it is hard to wait for the final judgment of your fate. Naturally, you become suspicious that your job is in trouble. By accepting that changes are happening and that they are out of your control, you choose to be on board with the facts. You don't have to like them, but you accept they are real. You acknowledge the truth without living in denial or sticking your head in the sand. Think about much more extreme situations you have encountered. Maybe you have family members who worship on Sundays, and you do not partake. You are all adults; they make their decisions, and you make your own. Once you accept what is, you can make the next choice. But it is very difficult to navigate through fear and other feelings if you are not pointed toward acceptance.

NOTICE WHO YOU ACCEPT AND WHO YOU DON'T

I'll refer to the wise words of Marianne Williamson in her book, "A Return to Love." She stated, "There are only two ways people converse or communicate. It's either *with love*, or a *call for love*." It doesn't matter if you are in line at the grocery store or sitting across from your mate over a candlelight dinner; all people want to feel loved. When others communicate with love, it's easy to love them back, even when they are simply dropping a receipt in our hand and wishing us a nice day! They're warm, kind, and smiling. You return their kindness with your smile. That is the act of love, not fear.

On the other hand, when people *call out or for love*, it's not very attractive. Yet that's when they need love the most. At times, it's difficult to give love because we feel reactive instead of accepting. Surely there have been many times when people have been outright rude towards you. We can't know what traumatic or painful event happened just before hand. Something awful might have knocked them off their game. When we take it personally and can't accept what is so, everyone loses.

Accepting people as they are takes practice. Patiently take a step back or take a deep breath and determine if the person is just calling out for love. What are you sensing below the words? Are they in need? If so, it is simply a call for love and if you accept this without harsh words or judgment, you will be aligned to make a good decision. You might say something thoughtful or offer a smile. You just might change the direction of that person's day.

In business, many of us have a tendency to be snarky, and really, this sort of attitude is the idea behind Williamson's idea, "A call for love." I have learned that in most cases, acceptance and a thoughtful reply has often turned the situation around. It's like magic. The person feels seen and understood. The trick is not to agree with everything, but to accept where one is at, what one is feeling, and respond without judgment. Try it out! See what happens when you relax and accept what is. Often the upheaval dissolves.

ACCEPTANCE DIFFUSED JUDGMENT

One of the great benefits of practicing acceptance is that your mind will diffuse judgment and negativity, creating space for other options. Practice with those closest to you as well as those you only see in passing. Take a deep breath and give recognition, validation and sincere love toward another – just do this mentally -- and watch your kind actions follow.

Don't fall into the other extremes and feel obligated to be best buddies with everyone. That's not acceptance. Sometimes I'll jokingly say in my mind, "I can love "them" but it doesn't mean we have to do lunch." Love is patient and kind according to the New Testament of the Bible, yet it is not a disguise for martyrdom.

A mentor of mine offered an amazing lesson while we were at a retreat having lunch with an older guy. To me, this guy seemed certifiably nuts. He was talking about how trees converse with aliens and that these aliens offered him a formula to cure cancer. He said numerous doctors were behind "his formula" and that they validated his conversations with aliens. He was literally "out of this world."

I felt fairly uncomfortable and looked to my mentor. She sat throughout the conversation with a smile on her face and acted like she believed every word. I was in awe. Later I asked her, "How could you sit there and buy into this man's story as if you agreed with everything?" She looked at me and replied, "Todd that's what he believes. That belief belongs to him, so degrading him or calling him a lunatic will do nothing. Questioning his belief will do nothing. He was having a good time. Who am I to judge or even suggest he is wrong? He might be right! How do I know?"

I remember that experience as a great lesson in accepting people and their beliefs. This was a guy I only knew in passing, yet the lesson about love and acceptance was important for my own development. My mentor accepted her story, not necessarily believing it internally, but she found a way to come from love by smiling and being a good listener. She modeled exactly what acceptance can do for people enjoying their afternoon and conversing over lunch. She showed me that we don't have to agree; answering a call for love often is a small and easy gesture of acceptance.

Practice accepting the way things are with acquaintances. It will quickly allow you to free yourself of negativity. You don't have to put attention or energy into things you can't change. Free yourself up and put more attention where you can make a difference and make good choices. If you stay wound up, worried about aligning with every thought and every person, you will live out of balance, and you won't have the clarity to make good choices.

NO ONE IS PERFECT AT LOVE RELATIONSHIPS

We don't have to be experts at romantic love to try it out. No one gets relationships right 100 percent of the time. Not even marriage therapists. Everyone makes mistakes. We begin with accepting the people in our daily or work lives while we practice accepting ourselves, and then on to the graduate class of accepting a mate. A person who's made mistakes and lived to tell the tale is one you can learn from more than a person in the throes of new love. Wisdom is really born out of heartache. Even little children know what it means to have their heart broken.

Like most, I was raised to think love endures all. It took many experiences to see that deep down, I don't believe all relationships must continue or that all of them are intended to last forever. I also do not believe we should use a person up for our own needs. People enter and leave our lives to teach us lessons. When two people enter a relationship happy and whole, they don't need each other as a crutch. Even if the romantic love does not last, both parties move on and understand that each are capable and kind. That's the power of accepting what is.

Being heartbroken temporarily is expected, but I have learned I must focus on learning what the relationship taught me so I can grow. Otherwise, it is too tempting to focus on what the person did or said wrong. This is not acceptance, nor is it loving to either person.

UNDERSTAND YOUR SOURCE OF LOVE

Create your number one relationship first with a Higher Power, whether it's Mother Nature, God, the Universe or anything that has meaning for you. It doesn't have to be organized religion. Not relying on another for your happiness or satisfaction in life is critical. People of all ages make comments like, "He doesn't make me happy" or "He's not doing what I want him to do." Neither life nor love work that way.

Relying completely on another for your happiness is a doomed plan because they'll somehow manage, without intent, to fail your expectations. Why would you want to hand that responsibility to someone else when it's your job to create your own happiness? Another person can join you in happiness, but no one is responsible for your happiness. Like many chapters from my life, I learned about this the hard way.

In my early sobriety, I wanted a girlfriend, and without being intentional about my needs, a woman appeared. Our relationship became serious very quickly. Unfortunately, I wasn't as discerning back then, and I discovered she was married. Remember my affirmation, "I'm always in the right place at the right time." I'd go to the grocery store and think she'd be there and as I parked my car her car was parked a couple of spots away. I'd think about her outside my shop, and a few minutes later I'd actually see her drive down the street. I was very intentional about her before I really knew her well at all.

I found love with this woman. It reached a point where she had to make a choice and she chose to stay with him over me. It broke my heart. At the time, I was confused about why I manifested her. What did my higher power have in mind? It was not clear to me then -- I needed to learn some life lessons about the difference between my ego and my highest value. Of course, I did not have a good understanding of how relationships worked. I spent decades of my younger years inebriated or high, which didn't allow for awareness and growth in my love relationships. This experience quickly brought me up to speed.

That was the first time I ever felt my heart was broken. I'd spent a lot of my life breaking hearts, but had no idea how painful it was to be on the receiving end. It was a lesson I needed to learn.

A LOVE AFFAIR WITH KNOWLEDGE

When you have a love affair with knowledge, heartbreak becomes a little easier to bear. I encourage you to have a love affair with learning about people and relationships. You don't know a person until you spend a lot of time with them. Don't be rushed and attach yourself to a particular person. Instead, be attached to the knowledge you gain from the experience. Relying on another person to be the source of all your happiness never works because they're human, too, and they have their flaws. My number one relationship needs to be with my higher power. That is my source of guidance – not my ego -- so all other relationships that come into my reality are true and real.

Once you can love yourself, validate yourself, and turn your needs to a higher power, you will be able to fully accept yourself, flaws and all. This is another layer of acceptance, and a very important one because none of us are perfect at love. We must accept ourselves even on our off days, and that helps us be ready to accept a partner. Life's journey is one of succeeding and "failing forward." Each time, we mature a little more.

CHOOSING A MATE

Keep in mind how the other person looks is far less important than building an understanding of how another person thinks and feels. There's much to consider as you explore the values of a potential mate and how they align with your own. Be open to the wisdom of people you trust and look before you leap. It is sad when people think they're in everlasting love together, and months or years later the relationship is a hot mess. Your first pro-active decision is to determine the type of person you want to share your space and desires.

As you decide what matters to you, beware of other people who think you should choose from their ideal list of qualities. For example, if your parents came from an academic, scientific or medical background where great emphasis is placed on formal education, you might feel that's important. But ask yourself: Is it really? Is this a quality I must have in my ideal mate? Of course, there's nothing wrong with education, but if you think it matters, it should be based on your values and not the goals someone else suggests.

There's also the idea that a mate with money is most suitable. Our culture worships riches and physical perfection, so it's easy to think a person who's drop-dead gorgeous and makes a lot of money is crucial for your happiness. Are they really? Chemistry matters, but chemistry isn't always instant. Attraction and love can grow gradually between two people as their values lead them to deeper intimacy. Over time a person you thought was average in appearance can become beautiful in your eyes. A person with a good heart who loves and respects you are always a better bet for long-term success. I don't suggest turning away from someone physically attractive, but inner beauty is far more long-lasting, and it is recognizable on the first date.

CREATE YOUR LOVE LIST

Make a 'Love List' of characteristics, qualities, and attributes you value in a romantic relationship. No one has to see this list except you, so it's not about trying to impress your friends or family. It's about what makes *you* feel happy and loved. If you don't know what those things are, take time to sort it out. Build a clear picture of your ideal mate. Generally speaking, the person you find will have the essential things you listed, if not more qualities that you will discover over time. That's why it is important to make time to consider your needs. Remember what you learned about manifesting? Acceptance is a choice – you do not have to accept anyone that you prefer not to develop a relationship with.

A good friend of mine went through the mill with relationships that didn't last. She was divorced twice by age 34. Then she got caught up in a relationship that became physically abusive. She pulled herself out and decided she needed to work on herself first. She was already a student of personal growth and spirituality, but somehow, she wandered away. After years of doing it wrong, she finally discovered how to get it right.

My friend learned to love herself and connect with Spirit. Letting go and trusting men was one of her biggest obstacles. She finally made her Love List. Her past choices were men she thought her parents or girlfriends would like. She carefully thought about the characteristics, qualities, and attributes on her list. She wrote only what would make her feel loved, not what would be cool.

In her words, her new partner would be a man who:
- Makes me feel cherished when he holds my hand
- Emotionally available and wants a committed relationship
- Shares my spiritual values and beliefs
- Has a good relationship with his family members
- Responsible handling finances and money
- Enjoys international travel and adventure
- Is a good listener and a patient person

Other ideas were just a bonus, but these were essential, and she focused on them regularly. A year later, she met someone who was a great fit because he had these essentials. They've been together almost a decade, and she still feels that deep connection.

I encourage you not to rush into anything. Experts on love say to take at least 18 months of regular contact before making permanent commitments. Get to know the person. If there are difficulties in the early days of your relationship, it is not wise to assume it will miraculously change. Sometimes the less experienced will risk it all and jump into marriage. Maybe they figure if it doesn't work they can divorce. That's true, but if children are born of your union, you're stuck forever dealing with that person you've severed a commitment with.

SEX CAN BAFFLE AND CONFUSE

If you're ready for a long-term relationship, don't jump in the sack right away. It's difficult to get to know a person when sex complicates things with powerful hormonal urges. You might want to shout, "I'm in love!" from the rooftops. Truth is you might be good together sexually, but not the rest of the time. Since most of your life is spent out of bed, it's crucial you're compatible in many ways, not just between the sheets.

If you're not interested in a long-term relationship and just want a hookup, at least be honest with your conquest for the evening. You may reach a point where you get it out of your system and finally realize there's much more depth in a true relationship. It's not all about sex, it's about having someone you cherish enough to share sex with. Sex adds a bonus, a physical dimension of pleasure to a kind, caring, and loving relationship.

To the women reading this book, there's a big difference between men and women. Okay, you know that, but I'm just sending a warning that most men have cavemen instincts and want sex at almost any opportunity. This is especially true when men are in their teens, twenties and thirties. Male hormones take over and deeply control how men think.

It may sound unfair – and I don't mean it that way -- but when a relationship starts becoming hot and bothered, women are the ones with the healthy brains and wise decision-making skills. It doesn't mean women are not feeling the heat. But even if he's trying to be cool and calm, he's feeling that testosterone-fueled drive. He has one thing in mind. If women can hold off on having sex, they'll find out how interested a guy is in getting to know her. The inner-caveman is close to the surface and wants to move toward pleasure, even if there are practical reasons why it's unwise. Women have a better shot at keeping their brain engaged and applying the brakes, so things don't go too far, too fast. Women, please consider building a friendship with your new interest. I'm not suggesting saying "no" forever, but if you can hold off from sexual encounters for a few dates, if not a couple of months, you have a better chance to develop a true friendship that won't be tainted by fantasy. It would be more politically correct to say both man and woman are responsible. That's how it should be in a perfect world. However, biology doesn't care about what's equal or fair. It just acts on that powerful drive to hook up.

OPENNESS WITH HEALTHY BOUNDARIES

In an ideal relationship, each person gives the other space to be unique, do their thing, and pursue their dreams. Good relationships provide openness with healthy boundaries. You shouldn't have to give up what you enjoy. Although relationships require some compromise, forcing or coercing a person to do something against their will isn't how to create long-lasting happiness. In fact, it creates simmering resentment.

My former wife was dedicated to attending church every Sunday. She was raised Catholic and that's what she did. That wasn't my thing and it became an issue that created strife. We could have talked about our values in this area before we married, and now that I've had the experience, I understand this is an important issue to share openly.

Other issues are not so big, and that's when you 'take one for the team' and compromise. You may do something for your partner even though you are not enthusiastic about it because your partner did something nice for you. Other times – those more important times -- you stand your ground. Deep connection and appreciation grows when two people in love compromise for each other. Learning to compromise is an exercise in acceptance.

Our culture encourages the idea of fixing people. You can't get in line at a grocery or drug store without noticing magazines with blaring headlines shouting, "How to make him more romantic!" Or, "How to make him help around the house!" But this is not "acceptance." This is focusing on conditions. Men sometimes become rescuers because they want to "save" a woman they see as a fragile damsel in distress and want be her strong protector. Likewise, women often choose men they can turn into a project saying, "He would be perfect if only..." Neither is unconditional love. Instead, both people are caught in limited trust toward the other. Grow to love a person as they are, rather than feel like you must change them. That's acceptance.

IS IT A DEAL BREAKER?

After a man or woman is treated poorly in a relationship, they often think a new relationship will fix everything. Hard to admit, but most of us drag some baggage to the next relationship. Most of us have a hard time putting ourselves on a time-out and reflecting before getting into something new. From my experience, deep change often happened while I was single. I needed time to be on my own, get focused, watch for opportunity, and not feel rushed.

Boundaries are important whether you are ready to start a new relationship or it you've been in one for a while. Don't be tempted to retreat and cave in the first-time new boundaries are tested. Observe your partner and pay attention to how she or he handles past relationships, family relationships, and even close friends. Observing provides key insights into how your future together might look. This will help you gain insight. Take time to consider:

- How does my mate talk about supervisors?

- What sort of relationship does she / he have with siblings or parents?
- What kind of person does she / he have as a best friend?
- Will hers or his style of relating mesh with my friends and family?

People who are exactly alike aren't necessarily meant to be together. Nor are complete opposites the best union. A person who helps you grow, learn, and who encourages you may be a more ideal match. Similar core values are important, but after that, a relationship can withstand some differences and still be a positive, loving relationship.

Project Everlasting was undertaken by two bachelors on a global traveling quest to discover secrets to lifelong love. They interviewed couples married many years to find the magic that kept them in love. Answers included compassion, understanding, forgiveness, and communication. An elderly woman married for decades looked at her husband and said, "Well, I haven't killed him yet."

You get a sense of couples who seem to click? They share little, private jokes. You see kindness and love in their eyes. A long-term, loving connection grows far beyond romance and sex to deep compassion and caring for each other. If you have ever watched an old sitcom from the 1950s, you see gender roles between men and women that are far more defined than in today's culture. He brought home the bacon and she took care of the house, the children, and had dinner ready when he walked in. Even though most people wouldn't choose to return to those days, many women have careers and still shoulder the responsibility of home life on their own. Boundaries at home have to change to keep up with how our lives have changed. When our roles shift, so must the boundaries.

When two people join forces, part of their relationship is a business. Writing a plan is a good exercise. What tasks will be delegated to whom? Always consider each other's strengths while you work out the duties. Spending time on it together may help you notice your vision is either aligned or different from your partner. Without a plan, you don't know what your partner thinks.

Even though we all have needs, don't expect your partner to fulfill every hope and desire. You can have friendships with other people to fulfill some needs. One friend of mine is a highly goal-oriented person. His wife isn't. When he tried to push her to get serious about goals, it created strife. He decided it was enough that she was supportive, upbeat, a great mom, and dedicated to making him happy. He's found a few friends who fulfill that need and they get together for power lunches or a game of golf. He has backed off from placing pressure on her now that his need is met. There are so many healthy ways to meet your needs without trying to change your partner. Explore how the two of you set boundaries and align your values – start with basic stuff and work your way into the more charged topics. The key is to include the values that matter most to you and hear out your mate who may have differing values.

And I must say this: Don't get married because it seems like the right thing to do. Don't give in to external pressure from family members who say, "When are you getting married?" Many people use critical comments and questions as fuel to "go with the program." The truth is that others cannot make these plans or decisions for you. That would be an infringement on your boundary.

Love relationships can be like living a dream or a never-ending nightmare. It's up to you to be the best person you can for yourself and another. Put your relationship with Spirit and yourself above all. Listen for guidance, and then choose the best person to share your life.

LIFE MASTERY KEY

#6

TRANSFORMATION

"There is no way to fail as long as you continue to learn."

~Dan Millman
Author of Way of the Peaceful Warrior

Anything is possible. My connection to Source and my daily practice of getting quiet allows me to know, not just think, anything is possible. As kids, few of us have a conviction that the right things are happening in the right order, at the right time, and will continue to happen without us forcing a solution. My relationship to my Higher Power offered a new faith so I could relax and get into the flow.

Much of this book is focused on personal growth and connecting with Spirit because I know it to be the way to bring the most joy and peace to my life. The same is possible for you. When you open up to the idea 'anything is possible,' and you firmly take action, you will see your plan or something even better unfold. That's the zone where amazing things happen.

FROM BROKE TO BILLIONAIRE IN SIX YEARS

In 2008 two guys in San Francisco couldn't pay their exorbitant downtown rent. Instead of getting evicted or moving back in with Mom and Dad, they got creative. They bought two air mattresses and rented them out on their living room floor for $80 each. When three people showed up at their door on the first day, they thought it might be a good idea for a business. They enlisted the help of a friend who helped them build a simple website. The business didn't take off at first and they were turned down several times by friends and investors. Finally, the tide turned when the drummer of a famous pop singer rented out an entire house for a week. The intrepid website was also supported by actor Ashton Kutcher who's known for having a smart business mind.

As people living in expensive cities learned about the site they discovered they could rent out a spare bedroom of their home or apartment and make extra income. As the idea caught on people in smaller resort and tourist towns started doing the same. Travelers learned they could stay downtown in the heart of the action in expensive cities for a fraction of the price of a downtown hotel room. The idea caught on and people around the world with rooms, apartments, condos, homes, boats with berths, and sleek, silver Airstream trailers started listing their unused spaces on AirBnB. As the concept exploded, the hotel industry finally noticed and started crying foul. But it didn't matter, the genie was out of the bottle.

Now travelers from college students to business execs, families and seniors check out the site as an alternative to traditional hotel rooms. In most cities, for the price of an average hotel room, you can rent a one- or two-bedroom apartment with a living room, a kitchen, a bathroom, and with much more square footage. For about half that price you can get a clean, private bedroom and bathroom in a home, often in great parts of the city. Who needs those fancy-schmancy lobbies and uniformed registration people anyway?

The company, born of two penniless guys who didn't want to give up their apartment, is now valued at $10 billion, which makes it worth more than Hyatt Hotels. They make money through a small service fee on accommodations all over the globe. But, the crazy thing is they don't own a single room. They transformed themselves from broke to billionaire's in six years.

Even when it seems to the skeptics that the evidence is flimsy, it still may be possible. As you open your mind and take action, you'll come to understand your capabilities extend on and on. Knowing this opens more doors to you. In the process of transformation there's an alchemy that occurs. I always thought of alchemy as a scientific term which meant to take completely different elements and find a way to turn them into gold. The ancient mystics, known as The Alchemists, in their quest to turn elements into gold were actually looking for "spiritual gold", which they believed was our understanding of self and our personal connection to Spirit.

Once that connection to Spirit starts clicking into place, you realize not everything is really about your ego after all. You gradually learn to put a throttle on it and get to work becoming the best version of you. Finally, you connect to your inner Spirit which is Source. Your connection will provide you with everything you need when you remain mindful and connected no matter what faith you practice, if any.

A huge transformation occurs when you start considering:

- What's my purpose?
- Why am I here?
- What really matters to me?

Using your gifts and talents is one way of expressing gratitude in your life. It opens the door of abundance. All the little keys we're given to open that door and lead to transformation, a better life, and a better understanding of yourself and the world you live and operate in.

ANOITED BY A MAGICAL WIZARD WITHIN

During ancient times, a wizard was known as a person of Source because they knew the life mastery keys to help others open the door and find a magical life.   At one time, a sorcerer, who practiced rituals and customs, was also considered a person of Source. Then, organized religion got hold of those ideas and restricted them. They saw it as a threat to their power and told their congregations it was bad stuff. As a result, they set out to discourage any journey or exploration that encouraged people to search beyond the holy book. Sorcerers and wizards were painted as dangerous people, not to be trusted. Organized religion sought to take away our connection to ourselves and our personal link with Spirit. It also sought to remove the powerful and significant value in personal growth.

Alchemists were exploring their own minds and hearts to understand the inner workings of what God truly was about. Alchemy is the transformation of dull objects into shiny ones. The true anointing is about turning dull material into gold in your heart and mind. You have much of what you need from the pages of this book to turn your life from dull to shiny and golden. You have the capability to be a modern-day wizard. Being a wizard in your own life is wonderful, but having a guide to get you started on your path of growth makes the journey a little easier.

Your mentor or guide is someone who can help you understand what you're experiencing. Having another person who's been down the path before you to bounce around ideas with and support and encourage your own transformation can be incredibly beneficial. Taking off on your own without support can be a lonely, spooky journey. When you start manifesting as a result of becoming the person you truly want to be, the changes can be massive. I'd like to be your spiritual mentor, a modern-day wizard, one who's gone before you. My purpose is to shine the light on your path so you can see it more clearly.

Start your journey by getting away from your negative self-talk and make a conscious decision to stop believing you're stuck. When you decide you want things to get better you'll start removing yourself from the daily upsets and your current stuck place. The process of transformation will gradually instill confidence and the wisdom to know it's time for you to try new things and get out on the edge of your own becoming. Only through personal exploration, self-growth, self-improvement, and understanding how the master keys work in your life does it all come together. When you get clear about what you believe by questioning what you want and what matters most to you, then the transformation will begin inside and outside. At first, you may have so many questions they bounce back and forth like a ping-pong ball. Gradually they settle down. Or, maybe you become accustomed to the bouncing. You keep pushing forward because once you've started, you can't stop.

As part of my journey, for many years I had a fascination with all things Egyptian. Whenever I came across information about ancient Egypt, I dove in and absorbed it all. As I began transforming and developing a higher understanding of spirituality and connection, I couldn't get enough of understanding the nature of wizards, alchemy, ancient beliefs, and how it all ties together. If you grab onto even a little of what's in this book and start practicing it, you will notice a positive difference in your life immediately. That's what transformation is all about. It leads you down paths toward interests and studies which will help you discover this amazing world.

DECLARE GUIDANCE THAT WORKS FOR YOU

If at first you feel disconnected from Spirit or a Higher Power I understand your reluctance, and I feel maybe you just don't know what you don't know yet. Whether you call it God, Spirit, the Force, Higher Power, Creative Energy, Allah or the Universe it is your connection to it that provides everything essential for living a successful and happy life.

Yes, we live in an ever-changing world. As I mentioned, I felt baffled as a kid believing the US was shooting rockets into Heaven and drilling for oil where Hell should be. Standard concepts for success taught for ages seem like they don't fit, don't work or don't make sense anymore. Simple ideas like, "Get a good education, a good job and grow with a company" are now almost laughable. Instead you may be part of the "gig economy" which provides a lot of freedom, but a great deal of uncertainty as well. Instead of smiling and saying "hello" to the people we meet, we walk around glued to our Smartphones while missing out on what's happening right around us. How do you navigate the landmines when your parents well-intentioned advice doesn't work anymore?

The Bible, still considered the infallible word of God by many, seems so outdated you might feel it's totally irrelevant and comically ask, "How can I believe that? How can that be?" It almost seems like fiction since it was written almost two millennia ago.

Whether you consider yourself Christian or not, there are rich stories and lessons found on its pages. Jesus was the most awesome teacher known to mankind and probably the most famous person to ever walk the planet. If you read between the lines of some of the passages in the Bible, they are connected to very metaphysical ideas and messages still highly relevant today.

TAKE YOURSELF OUT OF YOUR ROUTINE

I wanted to discover what's important to me and what I was passionate about when I started my personal journey and exploration. Getting away from my business and being with like-minded people who encouraged thought-provoking discussions gave me a chance to let everything else fall away. I discovered I could breathe, reflect, and let go. When I went through that time, I attended several seminars with Mary and other like-minded people, including shamans who taught from the Rocky Mountains of Calgary in Canada. It was an opportunity to leave behind routine and connect with my soul's voice.

I remember doing a meditation practice Native Americans do. They lay in a stream with their head upstream and feet downstream. They prop their head up with a rock. This was in a shallow stream with fast-moving water in the Rocky Mountains of Canada. I followed the instructions I was given carefully, got quiet and closed my eyes. The sensation of the cold water rushing over my body and past my limbs was like a metaphor for pushing away my previous attachments. I went deep within to the point where I was in such a profound meditative space I almost didn't feel the cold water. Afterward, I enjoyed an amazing feeling of a highly energetic frequency. You might not feel comfortable laying in a river or stream filled with cold rushing water, slippery rocks and fish. But you can let your morning shower be a time where you take a couple of extra minutes to feel the water slip down your body, washing away your cares and concerns. It's an excellent way to relieve your mind and detach from anything no longer serving you. Anyone open to change and transformation becomes a master at detaching from the unnecessary, if not sooner, then definitely in time.

PEOPLE OF THE EARTH, CAN YOU HEAR ME?

During this trip to Calgary, I had a moment of peace where I felt the magic taking place. Bear in mind that your defenses go down when you are in nature. I was much, more open to receiving messages because I had nothing to distract me and yet everything natural around me to use as guidance. The sky was constantly changing, and the wildlife was like a distant orchestra full of unfamiliar and unique sounds. In the midst of all of this, I heard a question that echoed out like waves of sound and light, it was: "People of the earth, can you hear me?"

I was very patient at this moment. It was like time was standing still. I understood that these words had everything to do with my calling to serve. I didn't know exactly what it meant – I just knew it mattered, so I made it my guiding mantra. I could feel my being tingle, and to me, this was more magical than following Bible verses. This was a guiding energy from Spirit, a direct message for me.

After leaving the Canadian Rockies, I returned home, but a part of me had changed. You will recognize this feeling in your own experience. As you trust that you are here for a reason, you will feel and receive messages that you cannot ignore and that you *don't want* to ignore! From this experience, I came to understand that I am called to light a fire in others. I am to serve in a way that helps people find a path they are especially passionate about.

Because I believed in this new mantra, I was introduced to people, places, and experiences that took me far beyond my daily life. The comments about my voice ensued while I was introduced to people in the radio business. Two years later, I had my weekly Internet radio show, Life Mastery Radio, which attracts thousands of listeners online to every show. Similar, "the people" heard me in Toastmasters and encouraged me to continue. I joined more clubs, and my roles in leadership promoted me to the District Director where I've become comfortable speaking in front of hundreds of people in a live audience.

I have left behind so many concepts and ideas I agreed to as a youth – ideas that belonged to my dad and step-dad, and the same is possible for you. The more you follow your own mantras, the more you know where you are going.

The origins of my story really are probably a lot like yours. We were all like sponges as kids, absorbing beliefs and ideas, whether positive or negative. We had a certain amount of programming indoctrinated in us by our parents, teachers, clergy members, and our community. You hold ideas and beliefs you never actually agreed to believe on a conscious level. Some of it was put in place to "protect" you from the big, mean world out there. Some of it happened because our teachers, whether it was Mom, Dad or someone else, struggled with their fears, doubts, and feelings of lack. Starting down the path of self-exploration begins to unlock who you are, why you're here and what matters to you. It's not about what matters to your parents or other people that's important. It's about what matters to you. Having support as you ask questions and seek the answers can make a big difference.

Your background and all the influences in your life may color your answers for a while until you start thinking independently and determine what's the highest and best for you. That's why transformation happens over time, and you may ask some questions more than once. After all, where you are in your head and heart may be completely different six months or a year from now. You'll see the world around you differently. Once you become more aware, there's no way you can go back, or as I like to say, you can't squish the toothpaste back in the tube.

A FIERCELY PRESENT MIND

Being in the present moment will make you unstoppable. You have the ability to recognize fear, set fear aside, and step into whatever you need to do anyway. That's incredibly powerful. You put embarrassment, shame, and blame to rest forever. On numerous occasions, when something important was coming up, I'd feel anxious and worry how to handle the situation. But after it was over, I'd think, "Wow, what was all the worry about? That was a lot of fun. I want to do it again."

Being present transforms your low or depressed vibe and offers a space of high-energy where people are drawn to you. They want to rise and be a part of whatever buzz you're experiencing and enjoying. Although I used to be the guy who sat sulking in the back of the bus during high school, I am now the speaker on the platform. That's transformation! Seems like I entered this world with leadership traits and somehow, I've always managed to be placed in leadership roles. I'm sure in the early days my ego pushed me toward high-profile positions. Now I believe it happens because that's the direction I need grow to stay on my path.

What follows is an awakened meditation, which will bring you into the present moment:

- Take a deep breath. Focus on powerfully, yet gently, inhaling through your nose

- Then exhale easily through your nose. Breathing through your nose is a Buddhist trick. Some martial arts masters teach breathing with a mouthful of water because you're forced to breathe through your nose.

- That simple breathing technique alone will bring you to the present moment.

- Once you focus on your breath, you're instantly right here, right now.

Using this awakened meditation has a peaceful, calming effect that works right away. Focusing on your breath alone is also a great way to start a meditation practice. If you get overwhelmed and caught up in your thoughts about the past or future, take a couple of deep breaths to bring you back to the here and now.

GRATITUDE IS NATURAL AND ESSENTIAL

If practicing gratitude is new to you, the first thing you want to do is start keeping a gratitude journal every day, writing down what you're grateful for. Another part of my gratitude system happens in the morning. My first thought is that I am grateful that I'm allowed to wake up! That helps set my mood for a great day.

I jump in the shower, and as the water pours over my body, a vision pops into my mind of being connected to the "all" with the water as the conduit. The water flows through pipes, goes out to the water system into reservoirs, lakes, rivers, and the ocean. Then the water goes into the clouds through condensation and rains down thousands of miles away. It's touching millions of others on planet earth as they take their morning shower, too. I'm spiritually linked to all, envisioning a powerful bond to everyone and everything. It's a cycle of water and a way I've anchored that connectedness to my life.

The third part of my gratitude system is I rely heavily depend on help and guidance from Spirit. You've already read about that throughout the pages of the book.

Some people believe in the idea of "fake it till you make it." Or, 'believe it until you believe it." Consider when you feel gratitude for everything that is and everything you want, you actually "practice the future." Give it a try, and you'll suddenly see more synchronicity magically occurring in your life. The more you practice it, the better it becomes. You'll soon discover you can never go back to who you were before.

The most prominent men in history understood that their ability to set the day in the right direction was a key for their success. Steve Jobs, the brilliant head of Apple who passed away in 2011, spent six weeks at a Buddhist temple in California where he got the idea for the iPhone. He said it was downloaded to him through his meditations.

All the great wizards of technology and science who've played a role in advancing our world like Thomas Edison, Nikola Tesla, and Henry Ford say they got their greatest ideas feeling connected to another Source which made them successful. The greatest discoveries from the most brilliant minds came from being present, silent, and still. They might not have used the word "meditation," but that's what they were doing.

"Everything that has happened or will happen has already happened." This was Einstein's theory. All those thoughts and ideas are available to us here and now. Through meditation and being present, you can tap into your inspiration. In 1905, Albert Einstein wrote all five of his greatest works in one year. He was intensely focused on solving problems. He was working in a Patent Office doing mundane tasks that didn't take much mental effort, but he allowed his creativity to kick in. He looked at patent drawings and would see they were mechanically sound and then start daydreaming. His mind would go to another place where he formulated new ideas.

Einstein had an amazing ability to be present and focus intensely. Newton was the same. They were connected to the present moment and able to articulate advanced ideas which made a huge difference in mankind even today.

When you're present how can you possibly be:
- Out of integrity with another person?

- Distracted as someone explains an idea or story?

- Anything but powerful in a humble way.

There's great power in presence and calm. Just understanding that and making it part of your daily practice begins a transformation in your life. Most of us miss the present because we are focused on the past or future. Being present doesn't necessarily mean perfection. But, the practices in this book will make a huge difference in how your life unfolds.

ALIGNMENT WITH PRINCIPLES

Getting in alignment with your purpose and accepting it with gratitude is when the floodgates truly open. Magical things start happening that may seem totally disconnected on your personal and spiritual growth journey. Pay attention, enjoy the ride and simply be in the mystery. Especially when the magic seems to require no effort. When you've been doing the work, miracles large and small have a way of showing up with ease. Those things happen in my life on a daily basis. Experiencing everyday miracles is my gauge to let me know whether I'm on purpose and on the right track in my life or not.

Every life is about finding the best way to be of service to others, in ways large and small. When you realize it's not about you, it's about making a difference in the lives of other people without a lot of recognition of fanfare, you're transforming. Going the extra mile for other people when they never know you're doing it truly is the mark of a person who gives from the heart and not for the glory. Never forget that you have the power to change other's lives for the better and in the simplest of ways. Just walking down, the street with a smile can make a difference to the people with whom you share your smile. You never know if one of the people you'll smile at is a surgeon about to do critical life-saving surgery on a child. Your smile brightens his or her day. The surgeon goes into the operating room with a better attitude and the procedure goes exceedingly well, saving a child's life. Or, maybe you smile at a person who was planning to harm another person due to their bitterness and anger. As a result of your small gift, they don't hurt themselves or others. Instead they decide maybe it's time to reach out and get help. You never know who you'll impact in a positive way.

PUT GRATITUDE IN YOUR POCKET

…. And take it with you everywhere you go! Gratitude is defined as "the quality of being thankful; it's a readiness to show appreciation for and to return kindness." It has a powerful connection to abundance. When you feel, and show gratitude for all the good in your life, you get to have even more. Gratitude is the mastery key of all.

You must understand that happiness stems from gratitude. If you're grateful and you assume an "attitude of gratitude," it automatically sends out a message of high-energy and happiness through your entire body. Every cell picks up on it. Some people say it takes 21 days to create a new habit in your life. Maybe that's why I was in re-hab for 21 days. Other people say it takes 90 days to start a new habit. Maybe that's why my sponsor suggested I attend 90 meetings in 90 days. It begins as a practice and when you gradually get in the groove of practicing gratitude, it becomes second nature and an effortless part of who you are.

Ask yourself: What am I grateful for today?"

There are times when my shop has become slow and I have people on the payroll who depend on their job to take care of themselves and their families. I want to make sure they're getting paid, which is dependent upon getting work coming in the door regularly. I always make sure I'm grateful toward each person bringing work to my shop. I am grateful they honor me enough to bring their machines in for repair because they know it will get fixed correctly and quickly. Each customer honors us when he or she brings in a machine or piece of equipment and entrusts us to get it working again.

A consistent, flowing daily attitude of gratitude basically programs your subconscious mind with a state of positive awareness and being. Some people wonder how it's possible to feel grateful all the time. How do you take what might feel like a negative right now and turn it into a positive? It takes practice, dedication, and a daily commitment to take ideas and events and choose how you'll think and feel about them.

When I started on my spiritual journey and read the book I bought at the airport, I had no awareness of gratitude. Being consciously aware and practicing it daily switched gratitude on for me. I was a bit skeptical at first but I figured, "Why not?" Shortly after rehab, I began a daily gratitude journal. Doing it regularly starts a positive flow of good.

When you begin your own practice of gratitude and consciously think about what you're grateful for, more and more good will begin popping up. This creates an energy feedback loop back to Spirit that says, "I'm grateful and ready to receive more." You can start out with basics:

- I'm grateful for having a roof over my head.
- I'm grateful for the food in my refrigerator and cupboards
- I'm grateful all the people I love are healthy.
- I'm grateful for my income.
- I'm grateful for my puppy dogs who are glad to welcome me home.

When you begin you'll start noticing positive energy changes Over time, you'll notice a radical change in how you show up and see the world.

BE GRATEFUL ENOUGH TO LET GO

A big piece of gratitude is about forgiveness. After all, how can you possibly be happy and grateful for everything if you're carrying around resentments and old hurts in your emotional backpack? Or if you're constantly thinking ill or negatively toward another person, how do you expect to feel grateful and free? Spirit will proclaim you're not ready for more or better if you are carrying old baggage.

Not forgiving can be a way of controlling or being right – and that is the absolute opposite mode of practicing gratitude. There will always be people who aren't having a good day unless they're having a bad day. In other words, they organize their life around negativity and something bad happening. But they are not your problem, and letting them get into your space will mess up your good vibration.

Forgiving the people who've hurt you is an important way of lightening your emotional backpack. It's a way of releasing all that hurt from your heart. As a result, forgiveness isn't necessarily for them, it's for you. Letting go of and releasing old hurts is a powerful way to allow more good in your life and make gratitude easier. Does it mean you have to accept the person who hurt or betrayed you into your life again? Certainly not. You can wish them well from a distance and know they're on their own path of growth. As long as you do not use this as avoidance or resentment, you keep the energy clean and you're back in alignment with your own transformation. Keep in mind that you cannot transform that which you are not willing to release. You want an attitude of gratitude to go with you everywhere!

Even if you don't see it that moment, understand there's a gift. It will appear even if it takes time. That keeps you in a good positive mindset and grateful for all the other good in your life. It takes practice, of course. Again, believe that I believe because it's never failed me and I know it won't fail you, either.

LET SPIRIT KNOW YOU APPRCIATEEVERYTHING

When you allow Spirit to know you appreciate everything you're setting into motion a change of events and you put yourself in the flow by expressing your readiness to receive more and more. You're grateful all the time for what you've received and you're also grateful for what's coming your way soon. You are affirming that you are ready to change and serve.

Are you ready to let go of the old thinking that got you here and rely on a new mindset? It takes a strong person to block out negativity. I had no idea what was next when I signed up for Toastmasters, started my radio show, and owned that my voice had a purpose, but I was grateful for all the possibilities. When I am grateful and present, things happen that I could never predict. The practice of gratitude, I believe, has put me in the right places at the right times.

From the time, I started speaking I had a vision of standing on a stage in front of thousands of people as far as the eye could see in all directions. My voice would boom out, "People of the world can you hear me?" A short time later, I became the co-host for a syndicated radio show. People were listening from not only all over the United States, but they were also paying attention from Great Britain, Australia, other parts of Europe and all over the world. It hit me the people of the earth could hear me, and thousands listened to the show each week. When I had that realization, I felt chills up and down my spine.

More recently I was appointed a top leadership role with Toastmasters International, District 2. It's my job to be on the constant look out for solutions and answers for groups in my region. I have a lot of ideas about it and I'm grateful for my role. It seemed like people weren't reading our newsletters. Nor were they getting the results we'd like to see from it. I decided we needed to do a better job of getting the idea of club quality out to the masses, so I began District Two Radio. People are loving it. They feel grateful for the show, so the gratitude is spreading. Now, other districts in Canada and in the United States want to know more about it. So, we're collaborating with other districts where I'm choosing several experienced Toastmasters to come on the show as my guest. I have one coming up soon to discuss mentorship. That's another example of being grateful and open to the possibilities. When those possibilities turn into opportunities, I take action.

What's remarkable to me is that gratitude spreads like wildflower. When you are grateful for what you have and what you are doing, those who can appreciate it will show up and spread that good energy with you. Each and every person in the world can contribute to others through the spirit of gratitude. It has been my experience that we are grateful once we've seen hard times and make new decisions. But I believe you can minimize the drama by taking action in your life and aligning with a power greater than yourself. I feel guided every day to serve and that comes from an attitude of gratitude. I've let go completely of the idea that life should have been different. Today, I know I am exactly where I am supposed to be when I am supposed to be there.

Once you experience an emotional and spiritual transformation, you can't go back. Compassion toward yourself and others feeds you. You learn to listen. You learn to completely accept yourself. You

126

understand you are here to be a success. You are part of something magical. You make space for the differences and the opinions of other people.

That openness will not just change you; it will change the world.

--THE END

www.ingramcontent.com/pod-product-compliance
Lightning Source LLC
LaVergne TN
LVHW051132080426
835510LV00018B/2362